JAINISM
NON-VIOLENCE & VEGETARIANISM

Compiled and Edited by

Dr. Tansukh J. Salgia
5540 Woodbury Hills Dr.
Cleveland, Ohio (U.S.A.) 44134

Foreword by

Dr. James E. Royster
Associate Professor,
Cleveland State University
Cleveland, Ohio

LIVE & LET LIVE
LOVE ALL - SERVE ALL
NON-VIOLENCE IS THE HIGHEST RELIGION

This publication made possible with the assistance of
Drs. Hansa and Vinod Sutaria of Cleveland, Ohio.

The information in this book has been compiled with utmost care to ensure accuracy. The publisher will be glad to receive your comments for improvements in a second edition, if any, but assumes no other responsibility.

Published by
Dr. T. J. Salgia
5540 Woodbury Hills Drive
Cleveland, Ohio 44134

Library of Congress cataloging in Publications Data

SALGIA, T. J.

JAINISM — NON-VIOLENCE & VEGETARIANISM

Library of Congress Catalog Card No. 87-91285

ISBN 0-9619706-0-X   3.95

Published in the United States of America

1st Printing 1000 copies

Dedicated to my respected spirtual teachers:

Acharaya Sushil Kumar Ji Maharaj (New Jersey)

Pujyashri Chitrabhanu Ji (New York)

Acharaya Balbhadra Vijay Ji Maharaj (India)

IN MEMORY

OF

MY

MOTHER

SAREKUVAR BAI SALGIA

PUBLISHER'S NOTE

All living beings in the world are moved by attachments and aversions, likes and dislikes and search for happiness in materialism. Everyone is restlessly seeking comfort while thirsting for love and knowledge; even the smallest living being aspires for superiority. But real happiness has never been found through the collection of more and more material things. How can it when it is not to be found there?

In the spring of 1968 I conferred with the head of a religious studies department (who has a Ph.D. in religion) at a small college in Tennessee where I was employed as chief financial officer. I asked about his knowledge and familiarity with Jainism. He did not know much about the relgion; however, he did ask that I provide him with some reading material. I wrote a letter to the World Jain Mission, Aligang, (U.P.) India, and asked for their support in providing me with material which could be used in the classroom. They were very prompt in sending many small booklets, which I shared with the department head. He was very impressed and at my request agreed to study Jainism in more detail. He also indicated that if possible, he would offer a course on Jainism at a later date. Since that time, I have been actively engaged in the propagation of Jain philosophy.

Many people in the West mistakenly believe that Jains are Hindus, or that Jainism is a branch of some other religion. It is not so. It has been proven that Jain teachings have been in existence since time immemorial. Jainism offers a unique gift to all mankind, namely the virtue of "Ahimsa" or the law of non-violence as it is called in the Western world. Non-violence is the strongest principle on which a moral world can be built for the bliss of all mankind and other living beings of the universe.

Jainism teaches that our material progress can be guided by the spirit of non-violence. And in order to achieve this goal, it is incumbent for each and every person to foster the sublime principles of non-violence. Only then will the heart of man change and peace and prosperity pervade the world. The practice of "Ahimsa" (non-violence) is a panacea of all ills from which the modern world is suffering; it is the solution to the conflicts between rich and poor, and between the Eastern and Western block of nations of the world.

My thanks are due to Shahu Shriyans Prasad Jain of Bombay, India, President of Bharatiya Jnanpith, for allowing me to use material from the book published by his organization. I am indebted to Dr. James E. Royster, Associate Professor, Department of Religious Studies, Cleveland State University, for his advice and also for writing the Foreword to this book. I am also thankful to Dr. Martin Plax, Director, American Jewish Committee of Cleveland and Adjunct Associate Professor, Cleveland State University, for rearranging the material and for providing other helpful suggestions. I am also thankful to Dr. Michael Tobias, Executive Producer, Maryland Public Television, for going through the manuscript and making constructive suggestions and for his moral support. I am also thankful to Lillian Morell for her assistance in typing the manuscript and proofreading.

I would be failing in my family duty if I were not to mention the immense help that my wife, Bharati, and ours sons, Anup Dev and Amar Deep, rendered, for their continous encouragement above and beyond the call of family duty in compiling and editing this book. Last but not least, I am equally grateful to those authors, historians and scholars whose books and articles have been liberally used to compile this book.

I have tried to put together the views of modern thinkers, philosophers, political leaders and religious scholars from around the world to prove that peace can be obtained by following the Jain path of non-violence. Notwithstanding my errors, if even a single person is inspired by reading this book to seek the truth in the right direction, I shall consider my efforts amply rewarded. Finally, I hope this book will arouse the curiosity of all readers to learn more about Jainism and take a sincere interest in its wholesome teachings.

Tansukh J. Salgia

5540 Woodbury Hills Drive
Cleveland, OH 44134
U.S.A.
October 14, 1987

TABLE OF CONTENTS

Foreword

Jainism, the ancient and indigenous religion of India, has exerted an influence in the land of its origin that far exceeds its relative size. With a current population of perhaps four to five million, Jains are vastly outnumbered in India by Hindus, and even by Muslims, a much larger minority. And yet, in spite of their relative smallness, Jains continue to contribute substantially to Indian life and culture, and are beginning to increasingly do the same on the world scene. This influence is due to at least three factors: 1. the profound philosophical system that ideologically undergirds the community, 2. the lofty ethical system that provides the framework for life, and 3. the industrious spirit and sense of responsibility that motivates action.

Mahavira, the historical founder of Jainism, considered himself — like Lao Tzu and Confucius of China — to be not the initiator of something new but the reviver of an ancient tradition. Born in 599 B.C.E., and an elder contemporary of the Buddha, he was the twenty-fourth Tirthankara, or "crossing-maker," i.e., one who has crossed over to enlightenment. His lineage reaches back to Ṛsabha who, though his origin is lost in pre-history, is identified in the early Vedic literature of Hinduism. And indeed, even Mahavira, the "great hero", and his immediate predecessor, Parsva, are referred to in Buddhist scriptures. The antiquity of Jainism as a teaching and practice is well established.

In spite of its ancient origin and long, illustrious history Jainism is little known outside India. This obscurity characterizes not only the popular mind but, though to a lesser extent, even the academic community in the West. It is a rare univeristy that offers an introduction to Jainism in its on-going curriculum. But the course of human events is contriving to change this.

History and culture on a worldwide scale have developed to the point where some of the teachings and practices of Jainism have become imperative if life, and especially human life, is to continue. Apart from invoking the universal principle that undergirds these teachings, as well as their corresponding practices, it is doubtful if global life can continue at all, let alone advance qualitatively. This eternal principle is none other than a profound reverence for life. While not unknown even in the West (compare Tolstoy, Schweitzer, King), reverence for life as it is propounded and applied in Jainism offers a means for turning the world around in its blind march toward self-destruction.

Jainism translates reverence for life into two concrete ways of living that are available to any conscientious human. These are non-violence, ahimsa (literally, "non-hurt"), the resolute refusal to inflict suffering on any sentient creature, and vegetarianism, the specific application of this principle to one's eating patterns.

Westerners may find themselves inclined to dismiss these two practices by arguing, on one hand, that they are negative in form, and on the other hand, that they are foreign to the Judeo-Christian tradition. Both arguments are spurious. To avoid injuring another living being and to avoid eating meat only appear to be self-denying because of socially prevailing patterns to the contrary. In other words, it is because a non-violent and non-carnivorous life contradicts the ingrained assumptions and widespread practices of contemporary society that it appears to be negative. It is, in fact, a style of living that is essentially affirmative. It attests to the inestimable value of life itself. The second argument is equally ill-founded. Non-violence and vegetarianism may be readily understood as but concrete applications of the Judaic and Christian doctrine of love, the unconditonal valuing of all forms of life into which God has breathed His breath. Even when non-violence is extended to the animal kingdom as vegetarianism it is but a wider application of the Golden Rule, "Do unto others as you would have them do unto you."

As human life becomes increasingly intertwined we have little option but to employ principles of living that are conducive to mutuality. Non-violence and vegetarianism, eternal verities of Jainism in particular and mankind in general, to the extent that they are increasingly practiced, insure not only survival but the progressive enrichment of life in all its forms.

James E. Royster
Cleveland State University

October 14, 1987
Cleveland, Ohio

NOMOKAR MOHA MANTRA

The Universal Prayer

NAMO ARIHANTANAM नमो अरिहंताणं,

Obeisance to the Arihantas - perfect souls - Godmen
I bow down to those who have reached omniscience in the flesh and teach the road to everlasting life in the liberated state

NAMO SIDDHANAM नमो सिद्धाणं,

Obeisance to the Siddhas - liberated, bodiless souls
I bow down to those who have attained perfect knowledge and liberated their souls of all karma

NAMO AYARIYANAM नमो आयरियाणं।

Obeisance to the masters - heads of congregations
I bow down to those who have experienced self-realization of their souls through self-control and self-sacrifice

NAMO UVAJJHAYANAM नमो उवज्झायाणं,

Obeisance to the teachers - ascetic teachers
I bow down to those who understand the true nature of soul and teach the importance of the spiritual over the material

NAMO LOE SAVVA SAHUNAM नमो लोए सव्वसाहूणं ॥

Obeisance to all the ascetic aspirants in the universe
I bow down to those who strictly follow the five great vows of conduct and inspire us to live a virtuous life

ESO PANCHA NAMUKKARO एसोपंच — नमोक्कारो,

This five-fold obeisance mantra
To these five types of great souls I offer my praise

SAVVA PAVAPPANASANO सव्व-पाव-प्पणासणो।

Destroys all demerit
Such praise will help diminish my sins

MANGALANAM CHA SAVVESIM मंगलाणं च सव्वेसिं,

And is the first and foremost of all
Giving this praise is most auspicous

PADHAMAM HAVAI MANGALAM पढमं हवइ मंगलं ॥

Auspicus recitations
So auspicious as to bring happiness and bliss

PEACE BE TO ALL

THE JAIN UNIVERSE

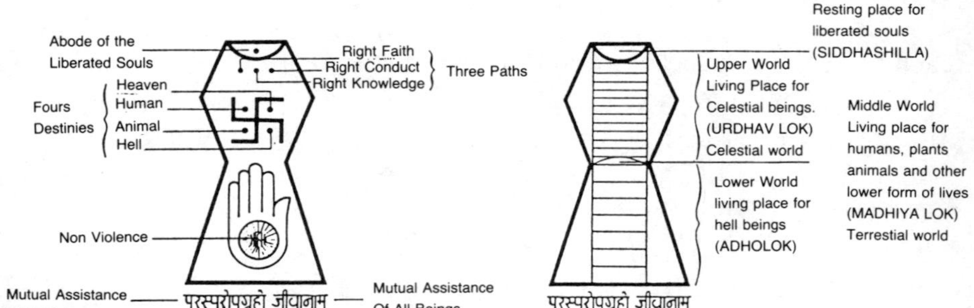

The shape of the universe resembles a man standing with his feet apart and his arms tucked on both hips.

> *The THREE WORLDS are shown in the human-shape. The SWASTIK represents the four states the soul may live in, viz, Divine, Human, Triyanch (Beings with three senses, e.g. Animals & Birds) & Hell. The THREE POINTS over the Swastik indicates Right Faith, Right Knowledge and Right Conduct. The HALF MOON indicates "Siddha Sheela", where the liberated souls live perpetually. The POINT OVER that indicates the liberated soul. THE WHEEL indicates Ahimsa. The Sanskrit sentence means "mutual assistance of all beings". The emblem symbolises that the wandering soul can, through Right Faith, Right Knowledge, Right Conduct and the practice of Ahimsa, achieve salvation. The Swastik Symbol adorns the Puja (prayer) Room in all Jain households.*

JAINISM IN A NUTSHELL

CHAPTER I
JAINISM IN A NUTSHELL

'Jainism' is the religion professed by the Jains, so called because they follow the path practised and preached by the 'Jinas' (lit. conquerors — of self). The term is an English rendering of the original Jaina-dharma or Jina-dharma. German Jainologists, like, Leumann, Winternitz and Schubring, prefer the form Jinismus or Jinism, which they consider to be the etymologically correct rendering. Both the forms are, however, correct, Jainism meaning the religion of the Jains and Jinism that of the Jina, although the former is more popular and in current use both in literature and common parlance.

Jainism is an important, fully developed and well established religious and cultural system, purely indigenous to India. It is the oldest living representative of that ancient Sramana current of Indian culture which was, in its origin, non-Vedic and probably non-Āryan and even pre-Āryan.

Dr. Hermann Jacobi, a German scholar of Eastern religions, and others are also of opinion that Jainism was related to the ancient philosophy of India, because of certain of its metaphysical conceptions, animistic belief, hero-worship in the form of worship as deities of perfected mortals, and of its being a very simple faith, be it in worship, rituals or morals. It has also been described as 'a very original, independent and systematic doctrine', of which 'the realistic and rationalistic tone does not fail to attract notice of even a casual observer'. Moreover, unlike many other indigenous religious sects, Jainism has succeeded in preserving down to the present time its integrity as a separate world in the midst of preponderant Hinduism. It is a complete system with all the necessary branches, such as dogma or ontology, metaphysics, philosophy, epistemology, mythology, ethics, ritual, and the rest, and is divided into several sects and subsects indicative of a long process of development. It has its own deities, gurus and scriptures, its own temples, places of worship and pilgrimage, and its own festivals and fairs. Besides devotees, it possesses well organized monastic orders, comprising both male and female ascetics.

The Jaina community, with its unique cultural heritage, has formed from the days of yore an important section of the Indian people and has been drawing adherents from almost all the various races, castes and classes inhabiting the different parts of this ancient country. In theory, Jainism admits of no caste distinctions, but owing to the growing influence of orthodox Hinduism in medieval times, its caste system came to be more or less adopted by the Jainas as well, though still not so rigidly. At present, the bulk of the community is confined to more than two dozen subdivisions of the Vaisya caste, though stray members of the Brāhmaṇa, Ksatriya and Sūdra castes and of several unidentified caste-groups are also here and there seen professing Jainism. The Jainas have for long abstained from active proselytization and there is no regular Jaina mission working in this direction, yet several Hindus, Muslims and Christians are known to have been converted to Jainism in the past hundred years or so.

Since the days of Mahāvira and the Buddha (6th century B.C.) till the advent of Islam in India (12 century A.D.), the creed of the Nirgranthas, Jinas or Tirthankaras, that is, Jainism, maintained its position as one of the three major religions of the country, the other two being Brāhmanism (Hinduism) and Buddhism. Even during that period it lost in members and many a time in royal patronage and popular support, due to the greater proselytizing activity of the Buddhist and of the Saiva and Vaisnava sects of Brāhmanism, which sometimes took the form of violent religious persecutions. Therefore, it went through the process of decline. A variety of internal and external factors made the community suffer both in influence and numbers, till at the present time it can count a bare four to five million souls as its members. No doubt, they form part of an elite and prosperous section of the Indian middle classes, are occupied in business, industry, banking, trade and commerce, the different learned professions, services and politics, and are scattered all over the world, residing particularly in all the big towns, capital cities and trade centres. The percentage of literacy and education is comparatively very high and that of crime very low. They are well known for their philanthropy, charitable institutions and works of public welfare. In their food habits, the Jainas are perfect vegetarians, rather lacto-vegetarians, do not eat meat, fish or egg, nor drink spirituous liquors. They follow, in general, such trades and vocations as do not involve injury to life, upholding the doctrine of ahimsa as best as they can, and avoid hurting or killing any living being. The members of the ascetic order, both male and female, are, on the whole, saintly, puritanical, selfless, possessionless, and austere in the observance of their vows and the rules of their order. The routine for the monk is very rigorous, and a speedier release is therefore possible. During the rainy season he seeks shelter in a monastery of the order, for then life is more abundant and movement pregnant with danger to it. For the remaining eight months he takes the road and wanders barefoot and bareheaded; he may not sleep in a bed nor take any conveyance, and may have as his only possessions his cloth, bowl, broom, and sacred books—indeed, these are not reckoned his own. He may not touch money; he must drink no wine, light no fire, and take no bath except in pure water. He may not disturb the insects or vermin which torment his flesh, nor do anything that may harm even potential life. Thus, monks are expected to walk gently, so as not to crush the living atoms.

The two principal sects are the Digambara (sky-clad) and the Svetāmbara (white-clad), so-called because the male ascetics of the former in the highest stage go about naked and those of the latter wear scanty, unsewn white clothes. Each of the major sects is further divided into at least three distinct subsects, the Digambara into the Terahapantha of Suddhāmnāya, the Bisapantha, and the Tāranapantha or Samaiyā, and the Svetāmbara into the Samvegi or temple-worshipper, the Sthānakavāsi or Sādhumārgi and the Terāpantha. The Digambara Terahapantha is so-called because it enjoins strict adherence to the thirteen (teraha) rules of ascetic conduct, and is more puritanical and austere, even in temple worship. The Bisapantha, on the other hand, is much more elaborate and lax in worship, and not so strict even in ascetic discipline. The Samaiyā or Tāranapantha is a medieval product, does not insist on temple or image worship, and possesses practically no ascetic order. The Samvegis among the Svetāmbaras are temple worshippers and constitute the majority. The Sthānakavāsis, who came into being about the same time as the Digambara Tāranapanthis, in the 15th Century A.D., are like them opposed to image and temple worship and instead emphasize the adoration of ascetic gurus. Buildings reserved for the latter's exclusive stay are called Sthānakas. A later derivation from the Sthānkavāsi sect is the Svetāmbara Terāpantha which differs from the parent creed only in certain ascetic practices and usages. The organization of the order in this subsect is more rigid and unitary, being subject to the dictates of only one man, the Ācārya or chief pontiff.

Certain misconceptions about the character, position, genesis and history of Jainism may be noticed prevailing among even some of those who are supposed to be educated and well-informed. Many a non-Jaina pundit, Indian as well as non-Indian, may be heard passing, cursorily, remarks like: Jainism is an insignificant, little known or an obscure minor sect of the Hindus, or a dissenter from Hinduism, or that it is a derivation from Buddhism. There are others who have failed to comprehend the Jaina philosophy of Anekānta, its Syādvādic mode of predication, the Jaina metaphysics and the theory of karma, or to appreciate the scope and significance of the Jaina doctrine of ahimsā. The cultural contributions of Jainism have not been duly evaluated, nor has the role of Jainism in the context of present day world problems been properly assessed.

Certain seals as old as, perhaps, five to eight thousand years, belonging to the pre-historic Indus valley civilization and bearing the figures of a nude yogin in the characteristically Jaina *kayotsarga* posture (perfect bodily abandonment) along with the bull emblem, as also the nude male Harappan torsos, seem to point to the prevalence of the worship of Ṛsabha or Ādinātha (the First Lord) of the Jaina tradition in that remote age. The rise of Vedicism, when the early Vedic hymns collected in the *Rgveda* were composed, belongs to a later period. In a number of hymns of the *Rgveda*, which is supposed to be the earliest known or available book in the world's library, Ṛsabha is alluded to directly and indirectly, as is also the case with the other Vedas. Besides him, several other Tirthankaras, who succeeded him, find mention in the Vedic literature, and the Brāhamanical Purānas have treated Ṛsabha as an early incarnation of the god Visnu. In the philosophical literature of ancient India, Jainism finds place as an important non-Brāhmanical system. The Buddhist literary tradition is no less explicit in indicating the prevalence of Jainism in times prior to the rise of Buddhism (6th century B.C.) — in fact, the last Tirthankara, Mahāvira, was a senior contemporary of the Buddha. Numerous epigraphical records, literary reference monuments and antiquities belonging to subsequent centuries, speak eloquently of the important and major role Jainism has played during the last two thousand and five hundred years in the life and culture of the Indian subcontinent.

As regards foreigners, Pythagoras and the Stoic philosophers of ancient Greece had certain beliefs and practices in common with the Jains. Alexander the Great is himself said to have come in contact with certain nude Jaina monks. Terms like 'gymnosoph', 'gymnosophist,' 'gymnetai' and 'gennoi' used by Greek writers beginning with Megasthenes (4th century B.C.) to Hesychois (5th Century A.D.), have generally been taken to have referred to the naked Jaina saints of ancient India. The Chinese pilgrims of the 4th to 7th centuries A.D. and the Arab merchants and traders of the 7th to 14th centuries were well acquainted with the Jainas and distinguished them from the followers of Brāhmanism and even Buddhism. The European adventurers and travellers of the 15th to 18th centuries do not appear to have noticed the distinction between the two communties, the Hindu and the Jaina, because, looking superficially with the eyes of a common lay and stray stranger from far off countries, there was none. The Muslim chroniclers of medieval times also generally suffer from the same lapse, but not all of them. Abul Fazl Allami's account of Jainism in his *Ain-i-Akbari* is tolerably full and elaborate for such a work.

Coming to comparatively modern times, Oriental or Indological studies by Western scholars commenced about the beginning of the last quarter of the 18th century. The credit goes to Sir William Jones, Judge of the Supreme Court at Calcutta, who took the initiative, pioneered the studies and founded the Royal Asiatic Society of Bengal in 1784 A.D. The first regular notice of the Jainas appears to be the one published by Lieut. Wilfred in the *Asiatic Researches* in 1799 and the contemporary existence of monuments, literature and adherents of Jainism was first brought to light by Col. Colin Mackenzie and Dr. F. Buchanan Hamilton in 1807, followed by H.T. Colaebrooke's 'Observations on the Jains'. This the most eminent Sanskritist of his times, whose personal 'collections' of Sanskrit manuscripts included a fair number of Jaina texts, gave a more or less accurate account of this religion together with a hint that it must be older than Buddhism.

As time went, the Jaina system of religion and culture came to be studied more and more intensively as well as extensively, and its literature, art and architecture, archaeological remains, tenets, practices, history and traditions became subjects of specialized studies. A host of savants worked in the field, most notable among them being Albrecht Weber, Leumann, Rice, Fleet, Guerinot, Wilson, Jacobi, Buhler, Hoernle, Hertel, Burgess, Jarl Charpentier, Vincent Smith, F.W. Thomas, Schubring and Zimmer. It is due to the sincere efforts put in by these orientalists and many others who drew inspiration from them or followed in their footsteps that now Jainology has come to be an important branch of Indology and Oriental studies, and a bibliography on any branch of Indology can hardly do without a reference to Jaina works on the subject, and no account of important religions of the world, or a comparative study of religions, is complete without Jainism being included in it. Its independent existence, greater antiquity in relation to not only Buddhism but even Brāhmanism, and the wholesome, abiding values inherent in its philosophy, tenets and way of life, with a universal appeal and message of peace and goodwill for all and every one, have become admitted facts.

VIEWS ON JAINISM AND AHIMSA

CHAPTER II
VIEWS ON JAINISM AND AHIMSA

In chapter one we explained the Jain philosophy in a nutshell, its basic principles, ethics and philosophy. Now we give below views of some Western scholars and Indian writers, philosophers and political leaders.

- 1 -

In Western countries, committing himsa (injury by mind, body or speech) is a commonplace thing. They are not at all disturbed in mind when they find men torturing men. Jainism is really a unique religion in as much as it preaches that all living beings should be protected, and Ahimsa should be practiced in everyday life. The Jains are very particular that no injury is done to any form of life when they eat, drink, walk or do any action. This kind of mercy we do not see in any other religion.

—An American lady in a speech delivered in Delhi,
India on May 4, 1953.

- 2 -

I am a Jain because Jainism presents consistent solutions to the problems of a happy life. The questions, "Who am I?, What am I?, For what reasons do I exist?," are all answered in the most irrefutable manner. It gives perfect health and peace of mind. There is a metaphysical and scientific explanation for all apparent injustices. Hence, I have accepted Jainism.

—Louis D. Sainter

- 3 -

Jainism is of a very high order. Its important teachings are based upon science. The more scientific knowledge advances, the more Jain teachings will be proved true.

—L. P. Tessitori, Italy

- 4 -

Lord Mahavira adopted a simple, logical, convincing, realistic and also scientific method of explaining the basic but universal principles of his teaching. He did not want to stuff the heads of the ignorant masses with mere symbols, rituals and images in the name of religious truth because his primary concern was not to present unwanted sophisticated mass of information to his hearers but transformation, a rationalistic change of man's defiled way of life.

—D. S. Parmraj

- 5 -

Let me assert my conviction that Jainism is an original system, quite distinct and independent from all others; and that therefore it is of great importance for the study of philosophical thought and religious life in ancient India.

—Dr. Hermann Jacobi, Germany

- 6 -

There is very great ethical value in Jainism for man's improvement. Jainism is an original, independent and systematic doctrine. It is more simple, more rich and varied than Brahamanical systems and not negative like Buddhism.

—French scholar, Dr. A. Guiernot

- 7 -

Jainism is really neither Hinduism nor Vedic dharma. It contributes to the advancement of Indian culture and study of Indian philosophy.

—Pandit Jawaharlal Nehru
Prime Minister of India (1947-64)

- 8 -

The beginning of Jainism and its history are much older than the Smruti Shashtras and their commentaries. Janism is completely different from Hinduism and independent of it.

—Sri Kumaraswami Sashtri,
Chief Justice of the Madras High Court

- 9 -

From modern historical researchers we come to know that long before Brahmanism developed in India into Hindu dharma Jainism was prevalent in this country.

—Justice Ranglekar, Bombay High Court

- 10 -

Instead of Jainism being, as was formerly supposed, an offshoot of Buddhism, it is shown to extend as far back as 3000 B.C. It is found flourishing alongside the nature-worship of the nude tribes in Northern India.

—Maj. Gen. J.G.R. Furlong, F.R.A.S.

- 11 -

Janism seems to be an indigenous product of ancient schools of Indian thought. Whatever the early savants of European fame have said to the contrary, it is to be noted that Jainism with all the glory of its Dharma and plenitude of its literature, both secular and religous, has been handed down from a hoary antiquity.

—G. Satyanarain Murti

19

With, however, our present knowledge of the Jainas and their sacred literature, it is not difficult to prove that Jainism, far from being an offshoot of Buddhism or Brāhmanism, was one of the earliest home religions of India.

—Prof. M.S. Ramaswami Ayengar

- 13 -

Jainism was the religion of the Dravidian people who were the pre-Āryan inhabitants of India. I am tempted to believe that Jainism was probably the earliest religion prevalent in India and that it was the flourishing religion when the Āryan migration came in India and when the religion of the Vedas was being evolved in the Punjab.

—Sir Sanmukham Chetty

- 14 -

The term Jain stands for self control and Ahimsa. Where there is Ahimsa the feeling of hatred cannot remain. It is the duty of the Jains to propagate the doctrine of Ahimsa throughout the world.

—Sardar Vallabhai Patel
Indian Nationalist leader and Deputy Prime
Minister of India (1947-50)

- 15 -

Ahimsā is the keynote of Jainism, a philosophy which comes from pre-Āryan days.

—S.N. Gokhale

- 16 -

No religion of the world has explained the principle of Ahimsa so deeply and systematically, with its applicability in life, as Jainism. As and when this benevolent principle of Ahimsa is practiced by people to achieve their ends of life in this world and beyond, Jainism is sure to have the uppermost status and Bhagwan Mahavira is sure to be respected as the greatest authority on Ahimsa. If anybody developed the doctrine of non-violence, it was Lord Mahavira. I request you to understand the teachings of Mahavira, think it over and translate it into action.

—Mahatma Gandhi (1869-1948)

- 17 -

The sages, who discovered the law of non-violence in the midst of violence, were greater geniuses than Newton, greater warriors than Wellington. Nonviolence is the law of our species as violence is the law of the brute.

—Romain Rolland

- 18 -

Whatever name we give to our creed, whether we believe in souls of animals or not, the noble words of Mahavira are the highest expression of human ethics. The great Law of Ahimsa, the Law of Non-violence, as it is called in the Western world, is the strongest fundamental principle on which a moral world order can be built for the blessing of all mankind.

—Dr. Alfred W. Parker

- 19 -

There is no religion on the face of the earth which does not honour the divine doctrine of Ahimsa — Non-injury and love. The remarkable feature of Jainism is that it has scientifically and elaborately expounded the whole philosophy of Ahimsa in such a convincing way that a novice can easily be the master of this sacred principle of life.

—S.C. Diwaker
Writer, Author and Thinker

- 20 -

The right of welcoming the delegates of the universal peace organization belongs to the Jains only. Because Ahimsa alone can contribute to the establishment of universal peace. And this Ahimsa doctrine was preached to the world by the great Tirthankaras, who were the propounders of Jainism. Therefore who else except the followers of Bhagwan Parsvanath and Mahavira can preach universal peace.

—Dr. Radha Vinodpal

- 21 -

Remember the teaching of Mahavira, the great apostle of Ahimsa and let non-violence prevail: —

> "Towards your fellow-creatures be not hostile. All beings hate pain; therefore one should not kill them."

—Mrs. Evelyn S. Kleinschmidt, U.S.A.

- 22 -

Non-violence is the greatest force at the disposal of mankind. It is mightier than the mightiest weapon of destruction devised by the ingenuity of man.

—Mahatma Gandhi (1869-1948)

- 23 -

The path of Ahimsa, non-violence, emerges unmistakably as the only effective counter to the atom bomb. The Jain message of non-violence can make a significant contribution in helping national and international societies to resolve conflict. More and more people have begun to appreciate the imperative need to adopt the non-violence formula so that a global war can be averted and tensions overcome.

—H.H. Acharya Sushil Kumarji
Jain Chief Pontiff, USA

It is imperative that the creed of universal love and practice of non-violence be accepted by the nations of the world before we stupidly hurtle into the atomic war of self-destruction. [Let's hope] Mahavira's teaching of universal love will shine and reign, which emphatically proclaims —

> 'Fight with yourself; why fight with external foes? He who conquers himself will obtain happiness!'

—Thomas H. Lawerence, Liverpool, England

- 25 -

Jain saints have a valuable role to play in saving the world from the grave danger of a nuclear holocaust. The entire world is facing the imminent threat of global conflict through the stockpiling of highly sophisticated weapons. And unless the healing touch of reconciliation is harnessed to resolve international disputes, the world at large might become a vast graveyard. All religions preach love and the shedding of hatred. It is the distinctive glory of Jainism that it has taken a lead in propagating the efficacy of Ahimsa. The Jains have set the pace in serving humanity. The glorious heritage of the Jain religion can benefit the entire world.

—Giani Zail Singh
President of India (1982-1987)

- 26 -

Ahimsa, non-violence, is neither dogmatic nor sectarian. Its foundation is not blind faith, but experience of various living aspects of life. 'IN THIS WORLD THERE IS NO RELIGION SO ALIVE, BEAUTIFUL AND KIND AS AHIMSA.' This Ahimsa is our heritage, our wealth, our spirtual light and our essence.

—Gurudev Shri Chitrabhanu
Jain Preacher, Writer and Poet

- 27 -

All the rules of conduct (laid down by Lord Mahavira) are based on love (*dayā*). Love consists in doing a kindness without any expectation of return, rejoicing at the prosperity of another person, and not being envious, sympathizing with those in distress and where possible helping to relieve it . . . . These rules are not commands. The Jain deity issues no commands. These rules are an aspect — the mode of behaviour of the man who practises them . . . . In my opinion Jain doctrines about life and the universe are the plain truth which, as far as I know, is nowhere else to be found. I consider them to be of inestimable value; without them I should not know what to believe.

—Herbert Warren, England

- 28 -

I think that Ahimsa as preached by Lord Mahavira avoids both the extremes — absolute passivity, which is impractical for the laity, and the wanton rule of might, which is thoroughly immoral — and strikes the Golden Mean, which is a path of progress for the soul to its final liberation.

—A. B. Lathe

If we really wish to understand the full significance of the doctrine — the lesson of Ahimsa that Mahavira taught with such remarkable success — we have to link up its history right from Mahavira and his predecessor Tirthankaras to Gandhiji and his writings and actions. It is only then that a full history can be written of this teaching which seems today the only solution for the present state of affairs in the world. Then only shall we realize what great seed was sown by Mahavira.

—Honorable R. R. Diwakar

- 30 -

The highest value which Bhagawan Mahavira, one of the greatest humanists the civilized world has ever produced, set for judging human behaviour is man's reverence for life in all its forms; no violence is to be intended, expressed or inficted through thought, word or act on any living being. This is known as Ahimsa. Similarly, though a prince by birth, Mahavira adopted a mode of living with minimum attachment for the world and its ties. He controlled his desires and put limits to his needs; thus he found solutions to various problems of life and death. Not only did he preach non-attachment but he lived a life which fully illustrated what it means. His preachings are meant for one and all who seek guidance from him. Intellectual tolerance, i.e., appreciation of the point of view of others, is the hallmark of his philosophy.

—Dr. A. N. Upadhye
Prof. of Jainology
University of Mysore, India

- 31 -

Today few things are more relevant and crucial to human progress than the Path of Ahimsa illumined, practised and taught by Lord Mahavira. Ahimsa is a dynamic concept. New aspects and new applications are continually unfolding with man's earnest, ceaseless quest. The incomparable example of Mahatma Gandhi has added a new dimension. His life was synonymous with pursuit of and experiments in non-violence and truth. It has reinforced to a degree unimaginable today mankind's strength and faith to follow the path of Ahimsa as a way of life.

—Dr. D. S. Kothari

- 32 -

At such a time (as the present), it seems to me that Mahavira's message of Ahimsa, Anekant, and Aparigraha is the only guiding light-house which can save the nation and humanity as a whole from ship-wreck in the turbulent ocean of life . . . . Mahavira's contribution to the national and emotional integration of our country can be seen in many ways.

—Dr. V. R. Nagar

- 33 -

The teachings of Jainism will be found on analysis to be as modern as they are ancient. The Jain teachers were the first and foremost in the history of human thought to propound the principles of Ahimsa, Non-violence.

—Dr. Sir M.B. Niyogi
Chief Justice of India

Mahavira, like the Buddha and the Upanishadic seers, has been a unifying force. The Indian historical sense differs from that of the West. To Indians the self-transformation achieved by Mahavira and Buddha is more important than are dates. The tenets of Jainism are of value in every day life; and the doctrines of Non-violence and Tolerance are applicable in international politics and are of importance for peaceful coexistence.

—Prof. N.A. Nikam

- 35 -

Jainism has contributed to the world the sublime doctrine of Ahimsa. No other religion has emphasized the importance of Ahimsa and carried its practice to the extent that Jainism has done. Jainism deserves to become the universal religion because of its Ahimsa doctrine.

—Dr. Rajendra Prasad
President of India (1950-1962)

- 36 -

Mahavira proclaimed in India the message of salvation that religion is reality and not a mere convention, that salvation comes from taking refuge in the true religion and not from observing the external ceremonies of the community, that religion cannot regard any barriers between man and man as an eternal verity. Wondrous to say, this teaching rapidly overtopped the barriers of the race's abiding instinct and conquered the whole country.

—Sir Rabindranath Tagore (1861-1941)
Poet, Philosopher, Nobel Laureate

- 37 -

In short, believers in the creation theory make God a man, bring him down to the level of need and imperfection; whereas Jainism raises man to Godhood and inspires him to raise himself as near to Godhood as possible by steady faith, right perception, perfect knowledge and, above all, a spotless life.

—Dr. Mohammad Hafiz, Ph.D., D.Lit.

- 38 -

Well, then, what is the Light left in our custody by Lord Mahavira? . . . Briefly characterised the Light teaches us, [1] Spiritual independence which connotes individual freedom and unlimited responsiblity. The soul depends upon none else for its progress, and none else is responsible for the degradation and distress which the soul may be affected with . . . . [2] It teaches us the essential universality of the Brotherhood of not only all men but of all that lives. The current of life in the lowest living organism is as sacred, subtle, sensitive, mighty and eternal as in Juliet, Cleopatra, Caesar, Alexander, Christ, Muhammad, and Lord Mahavira himself. This is the undying basis of our fraternity for all.

—Prof. J.N. Farquhar

No scholar, I think, will deny that Jainism is one of the greatest and most important creations of the Indian mind, still surviving after centuries of glorious life. There is no branch of Indian civilization or literature or philosophy on which the deeper study of Jainism will not throw light. It is impossible for any sound scholar interested in the history of Indian logic to ignore Jain logic, which deserves the largest attention and most diligent researches . . . . The literature of every belief can be discussed and scrutinized by scholars, but the living essence of Mahavira's doctrine shall remain untouched by any criticism.

—Dr. G. Tucci, Italy

- 40 -

The Jains have created a system of metaphysics, minutely developed, which in its terminology as also its content, could be looked upon as an independent and unique product in the philosophical systems of the wonderfully fruitful Indian spirit.

—Dr. Helmuth Von Glasenapp,
Professor, Berlin University, Religious Studies

- 41 -

I look with considerable appreciation upon Jain logic as having long distinguished principles which only now are being re-discovered in the West.

—Dr. Archie J. Bahm,
Professor, University of New Mexico

- 42 -

Man's progress has always been due to the efforts of some highly spiritual personalities who have graced the earth with their presence now and then. Such outstanding personalities are not necessarily born in one country or at one time. Yet the work of them all is ultimately to make the world happier by making man conscious of his duties toward those among whom he lives. Mahavira was one of these great teachers of humanity. The doctrine of non-violence, mercy and forbearance reached in Mahavira's teachings its highest expression.

—M. S. Aney

- 43 -

Thus Mahavira appears in the tradition of his own sect as one who, from the beginning, followed a religion established long ago; had he been the founder of Jainism, tradition, ever eager to extol a prophet, would have totally expressed his claims to reverence, as such. Nor do Buddhist traditions indicate that the Nirgranthas owed their origin to Nathaputta; they simply speak of them as of a sect existing at the time of Buddha. We cannot, therefore, without doing violation to tradition, declare Mahavira to have been the founder of Jainism.

—Dr. Hermann Jacobi, Germany

The Gospel of Ahimsa was first deeply and systematically expounded and properly and specially preached by the Jaina Tirthankaras, most prominently by the 24th Tirthankara, the last one, Mahavira Vardhamana. Then again by Lord Buddha. And at last it was embodied in the thoughts, words, deeds, and symbolized by the very life of Mahatma Gandhi.

—Prof. Tan Yun-shan, China

- 45 -

The Jainas themselves regard Mahavira not as the first but as the last of their long series of Tirthankaras. The traditional number is 24 . . . . Such an ascetic is termed a 'hero' [Vira]; that is the sense of the title Mahavira, the great [mahat] hero [vira] which has been bestowed on the Buddha's contemporary, Vardhamana, the 24th Tirthankara. The saint is also termed Jina, the 'Victor', and his disciples, therefore, Jainas, the followers of the Victor.

—Dr. Heinrich Zimmer
German Indologist

- 46 -

Through His Jnana and the creed of Ahimsa, Mahavira destroyed the world of the materialistic creed and ethics in a way that we may call Him a Superman of the first kind: We claim for Him the verses of the German Thinker, Herder —

> He's hero, the conqueror of battlefields,
> He's hero, the conqueror in lion hunting,
> But He's Hero of Heroes', the conqueror of
> Himself!

—Joseph Marie, Bonn, Germany

- 47 -

The name of Mahavira and Ahimsa culture is replete with peace unutterable, the Bliss embodied in such seed-name vibrations. Holy, Holy, Holy art Thou Mahavira and Thy Conquests. The example of Thy Victory is the measure for which mankind, and indeed all life imprisoned in matter, can aspire.

—Dr. William Henry Talbot, England

- 48 -

The teachings of Mahavira sound like the triumphal song of a victorious soul that has at last found in this very world its own deliverance and freedom —. The Religion by Him so modified became the religion of absolute coherence, the most precise, straight, perfect doctrine.

—Dr. Alberto Poggi, Italy

The most striking feature in the genius of Mahavira from the psychological point of view is the tremendous will power which characterizes every act of his career during the most significant century in the history of human thought. Deliberately, without a single moment of hesitation or doubt, Mahavira proceeds to demonstrate in his own example how the human mind can be disciplined and controlled in such a way that the highest intellectual and spiritual level can be attained in a single life-time.

—Dr. Felix Valyi

We should try to develop a spirit of global humanism based on a fusion of and a collaboration between religion and humanism so that religion can provide the necessary philosophical and spiritual foundation for peace under the banner of Ahimas, non-violence. There is no discrimination between one race and another because it advocates that all living beings should be treated as deserving our equal love.

—H.H. Charukeerthi Bhattaraka Swamiji,
Shravanabelogola, India

One of the most prominent features of Lord Mahavira's personality seems to me to have been an endless energy (Ananta Virya) by means of which the famous Tirthankara, as it were, forced his way through His contemporaries. Before his advent, people and even ascetic orders, as is stated in Buddhist sources, were 'living in incontinency (*abrahmacaryavāsa*)'. As for the Vedic Brahmans, they were not so strict in matters of sexual pleasures . . . . The great strength of the Great Hero Vadhamana manifests itself also in the most rigorous penances. He practised with a resolute heart, as when He stripped himself of every sort of cloth and adpoted the observance of absolute nakedness. Holy life, not only holy words, was His constant rule.

—Dr. Ferdinando Belleni-Fillippi

If we, men of western origin, do not find this way (to salvation — the solution to the problem of the mechanised occidental world) ourselves, we should open our hearts to the messages of the East, where India has grown fit to become the home of the spiritual humanism, where Tirthankara Mahavira proclaimed; "Towards your fellow creatures be not hostile. All beings hate pain: therefore do not kill them."

—Walter Leifer, Germany

Liberation of the soul from the shackles of the body was accomplished by the supreme Lord Mahavira, the last of the twenty-four world teachers of Jainism . . . . He, by his great power and soul-force, inspired the souls of entire provinces to heights of pure love, peace, understanding and joy, unknown in this world since the days of the preceding Tirthankara, Lord Parshvanatha. Poverty, fear, misunderstandings, envy, lust, were all swept away by the awesome vibrations of his magnetic soul. The sight of the Tirthankara is a sufficient answer to the question — 'Where is happiness?' His teachings constitute the way of liberation, and are the greatest of all contributions to human welfare. His footprints, for all to follow, lead to Nirvana, where the soul lives eternally in perfection of joy, perception, knowledge and power. During the thirty years when he was a world teacher, Mahavira proclaimed the truth that man is the master of his own destiny — the Jina or conqueror. To refrain from killing and injuring is the only true religion. The greatest gift that man can make to his fellowmen and the lower creatures is the gift of protection and safety, that they shall come and go without harm or interference.

—W. George Trott, England

- 54 -

Mahavira was called Nigrantha because he was outwardly unclothed and inwardly free from all worldly bonds and ties. And it is not surprising at all that he should be described in Buddhist literature as 'the head of an Order, of a following, the teacher of a school, well-known and of repute as a sophist, revered by the people, a man of experience who has long been a recluse.'

Those who came under the influence of Mahavira's personality and teachings gave up the eating of meat and fishes for good, and adhered to a vegetarian diet.

Salvation was preached (by Him) as the birth-right of men; and it was assured to all without distinction of caste or creed or sex.

—Dr. B. C. Law

- 55 -

I think it was the tremendous force let loose by Lord Mahavira that really created Lord Buddha. I personally believe that if Jainism had kept its hold firmly in India, we would have had a more united India and certainly a greater India than today.

—Sir Sanmukham Chetty

- 56 -

Lord Mahavira wiped out all the passions forever and could therefore perceive and practice truth — whole truth, though multifarious, and of which an ordinary man can hardly see even one face or aspect. This truth is reflected in toto in his general sermons which have for their adamantine basis the two eternal principles of *anekantvada* and *ahimsa*.

—Prof. Hiralal R. Kapadia

- 57 -

Sri Vira [Mahavira] from his very childhood was of an extremely unaggressive and non-acquiring disposition. The spirit of renunciation was a marked trait in his character and made it possible for him not only not to hanker after worldly possessions but to give away even what he had. His life shows the fundamental principle upon which socialism is to be founded and the way in which its aim and ideal can be progressively worked out unquestionably. He is the transcendant ideal, to be followed as much faithfully and as much closely as possible.

—Dr. Harisatya Bhattacharya

- 58 -

Lord Mahavira, who was the last in a long series of Jain savants believed to go back to the dawn of civilization, was a personality of great power and radiance. His impact is by no means confined either to those who specifically call themselves Jains or to the boundaries of India. Through the ages eminent thinkers from various parts of the world have studied Lord Mahavira and his teachings and have commented upon them from their own special view points.

—Dr. Karan Singh

- 59 -

Mahavira was deeply influenced by the democratic ethos of the society in which he was brought up. He was also impressed by the inadequate application of this ethos in the political, economic and social life of the community without its being based upon a really democratic religious system, so that he took it upon himself to work out and propagate a system of complete spiritual democracy.

—Dr. Amar Chand

- 60 -

It is due to his rare qualities as an ideal reformer, an able organizer, a patronizing guru, a convincing debator, a zealous missionary, and an upholder of the equalty of all human beings that the name of Lord Mahavira still remains and shall ever remain a cherished inspiration to humanity at large. It has been well over two and a half thousand years since the personality of Lord Mahavira illuminated the religious horizon of India. And yet with the passage of several centuries, the influence of his teachings, instead of waning, as happened in the case of several others, is on the increase.

—Dr. S. B. Deo

- 61 -

In socialism all are given opportunities and any person can aspire to be a great person by his efforts. Mahavira's life is a true testimony to this principle enunciated today . . . . Mahavira belonged to the class of sages and saints who did sympathize with the sufferings of the poor and down-trodden and did serve humanity by their sincere and pious deeds . . . . He preached a philosophy by which social order may be established on the firm foundations of universal love, universal brotherhood, and the spirit of altruism, which are the basic principles of socialistic discipline of any age and of any country.

—Dr. P. M. Upadhye

- 62 -

Full and complete knowledge based on right faith and translated into right conduct coupled, at the same time, with complete non-attachment to non-soul matters was considered by Lord Mahavira as a condition precedent for the final release of the soul from the bondage of world life.

—L. A. Phaltane

29

Mahavira is not the founder of Jainism. He revived the Jaina doctrines. He was more a reformer than the founder of the faith. He was the 24th Tirthankara and the first active propagator.

—Swami Shivananda

- 64 -

Lord Mahavira again brought into prominence the doctrine of Jainism. Jain religion was prevalent in India before Buddhism. In ancient times innumerable animals were butchered in sacrifice. The credit for the disappearance of the massacre from the Brahmanical religion goes to the share of Jainism.

—Bal Gangadhar Tilak (1856-1920)
Freedom Fighter of India

- 65 -

Lord Rishabhadev belonged to the Ikshvaku clan. Swami Samant Bhadra in Swayambhu Stotra says: —

Rishabha was the first person of Ikshavaku clan. This establishes the fact that the Vedic literature regards Rishabhadev as a great soul, who flourished long before the Vedas were compiled . . . The 15th Vaman Avatara has been mentioned in the Rigveda. Rishabhadeva was the ninth Avatara, therefore the period of Rishabhadeva is much prior to the composition of Vedas. This goes to prove that the founder of Jainism, Lord Rishabha, belonged to Pre-Vedic period. The Lord taught the message of Mercy and Love to humanity long before Krishna, who was the 23rd Hindu Avatara.

—Swami Samant Bhadra

- 66 -

Jain literature is of great importance for our knowledge of the ancient literature of India. Jainism contains a vast mine of knowledge that is well worth exploring by all who are interested in the history and culture, both philosophic and religious, of ancient India.

—Dr. Hermann Jacobi, Germany

- 67 -

A passage in the Rigveda reads as follows: "Says the Yajaman, 'We favor the naked gods who are holy and who purify others'."

A passage in the Yajurveda XXV, 19, contains the names of the three Jain Tirthankaras, viz, *Rishabha, Ajitanath* and *Aristanemi.*

In the Samaveda, there is a reference to a Yati who condemned animal sacrifices. Obviously, he must be no other than a Jain.

In the Rigveda, people are mentioned who lived in Magadha (presently in the state of Bihar, India) and who condemned animal sacrifices.

Bhagwan Veda Vyas says in the Brahma Sutra that two aspects of one thing are not possible. On the contrary, the theory of relativity (Anekantvada) is peculiar to the teachings of Jainism.

—Passages from Hindu Scriptures

- 68 -

Sri Sankaracharya has done injustice to this system (of Syadvada) by not understanding it properly. Many learned scholars after him also subscribed to his views. It is to be understood that the great Maharishi thought it unnecessary to see the original works on this system (otherwise he would not have misunderstood Jainism.).

—Professor Phanibhushan Adhikari,
Hindu University, Benares, India

- 69 -

We are reminded of the antiquity of Jainism when we study the things obtained from the excavations at Mohen-jo-daro, ancient inscriptions, caves and many ancient ruins.

Jainism began when this world began. I am of the opinion that Jainism is much older that the Vedic darshana.

—Swami Ram misraji Shastri
Professor, Sanskrit College, Benares

- 70 -

"There is nothing unusual in my saying that Jainism was in existence long before the Vedas were composed."

—Dr. S. Radhakrishnan,
President of India (1962-67)

- 71 -

The first poet of the Kannada language was a Jain. The credit for writing the ancient and the best literary works goes to the Jains.

—R. B. Narasimhacharya

- 72 -

We learn from Sashtras and commentaries that Janism is existing from beginningless time. This fact is indisputable and free from difference of opinion. There is much historical evidence on this point.

—Bal Gangadhar Tilak (1856-1920)
Freedom Fighter of India

Bhagawan Mahavira taught Jainism again. He was the twenty-fourth avatara (incarnation). Before him there were twenty-three avataras such as Rishabha, Nemi, Parsva etc. They also propagated Jainism. In this manner there was Jainism existing even before these twenty-three avataras. From this the antiquity of Jainism is established.

—Bal Gangadar Tilak (1856-1920)
Freedom Fighter of India

- 74 -

Hindu culture is a part of Indian culture. Jain and Buddhist cultures are also Indian. They are not (parts of) Hindu culture.

—Pandit Jawaharlal Nehru
Prime Minister of India (1947-1964)
(Discovery of India)

- 75 -

What will be the condition of the Indian Sanskrit literature if the contributions of the Jains are removed? The more I study the Jain literature the more happy and wonderstruck I am.

—Dr. Hertel, Germany

- 76 -

In the field of history, Jain history is the most useful of all for the world. It is very helpful to those who write histories and to those who study the old inscriptions and other monuments.

—Dr. Satischandra, M. A., Ph.D.

- 77 -

The Jain Sadhu leads a life which is praised by all. He practices the vratas and the rites strictly and shows to the world the way one has to go in order to realize the atma. Even the life of a Jain householder is so faultless that India should be proud of him.

—Dr. Satischandra, M.A. Ph.D.

- 78 -

Whoever in life has attained the proper intuitive knowledge sins no more. He sees, like Mahavira, all deities at his feet, and is all-knowing. Mahavira's is the (earthly) final state which the perfect ascetic enters and is also called *nirvana [jivan-mukti]*.

—Max Weber, Germany

Jains offer their message to all. In Jainism you will not be requested to accept any statement with blind faith. From my personal experience, I can say that all who will accept its teachings and put them into practice will enter a world of undreamed delight.

Jainism teaches that soul is immortal and in its pure nature is full of absolute knowledge and infinite bliss. It is only when soul is drawn low by the body and the senses that it is held in bondage with karmas. To meditate for only a few minutes daily on the pure nature of the soul is a path to Liberation and Salvation. These are the main reasons why I accepted wonderful Jainism.

—Matthew Mckay, England

- 80 -

What is the use of creating new religious movements, when Jainism could offer the Solution required for the needs of suffering man-kind. It has the advantage of possessing an ancient and venerable tradition. It is the first amongst the world religions which proclaimed Ahimsa as the main criterion of moral life.

—Dr. Louis Renou, Professor, Sorbonne
University, Paris

- 81 -

This miserable world may become paradise, with all and all peace, everlasting joy and true infinite bliss, if Jainism is practiced by all the people of the world.

—Dr. Charlotta Krouse

Jainism teaches and respects the right of all beings to live in peace. It does not distinguish between the willful murder of innocent humans and the willful killing of harmless creatures. Non-violence is the highest religion.

JAINISM, VEGETARIANISM and HEALTH

CHAPTER III
JAINISM, VEGETARIANISM and HEALTH

Now let us investigate the conditions prevailing in the world which have caused so much unrest and chaos. For our purpose, it is necessary to survey the activities of the individual man and thereby ascertain how far spiritual awakening in the light of Ahimsa has influenced his primary instincts in daily life. Let us begin from his food instinct. Man requires food for the upkeep of a healthy body, but today food has become a luxury to satisfy the relishes of the tongue. Void of Viveka, not heeding the inner voice of conscience and caring little for Ahimsa, man, devours whatever is placed before him in a fashionable way and is appealing to his taste. People care but little to ascertain whether the food they take is natural and not harmful. Nobody seems to remember that man is a herbivorous living being and his right food is corn, fruit and vegetable. Prominent medical opinion declares it so. To begin with, Sir Henry Thompson, M.D., F.R.C.S., writes:

"It is a vulgar error to regard meat in any form as necessary to life. This statement is amply proved by the fact that three-fourths of the human race do not eat flesh. It is difficult to understand how a civilisation can call itself Christian or humane or even rational, while its main article of food is not only unnecesary but more than that involves so much degration to the producer, disease to the consumer, and untold suffering and cruelty to the victims."

Likewise another medical authority, Dr. Josiah Oldfield remarks:

"In order to secure a clear head upon an active body, I am of the opinion that a man should give up eating all dead bodies and all preparations of them — all entrails, organs, muscles, blood and bones of dead animals, under whatever fancy names they may be presented and should carefully and wisely select from the products of the field, harvest the garden, the orchard and the forest."

Vegetarian diet is helpful to health and prolongs life. The opinion of Dr. John H. Kellog, M.D., LL,D. is worth perusal. He writes:

"There is nothing necessary or desirable for human nutrition to be found in meats or flesh foods which is not found in and derived from vegetable products."

But in spite of such eminent medical opinion in favour of vegetarian food, most of our intelligentsia is swayed away with the alluring tastes of the meat dishes. They believe in Ahimsa yet eat the carcasses of animals. Does it not cause pain and fear to lesser brethren, the animals? When one hurts life, how can he style himself an Ahimsaist? But the wonder is that a few of the modern pacifists, who are so very anxious and are true in their laudable efforts to establish peace in the world, do not attach much importance to diet reform. Explaining the difference in the approach between Western and Gandhian pacifisms, Rev. John Nevin Sayre, an American representative to the World Pacifist's Conference held at Wardha (India), said:

"I think our pacifism would be very close to Ahimsa, with this difference. I think Ahimsa would involve refusal to take any life including animal life. Our pacifism does not go that far. The kind of pacifism I am talking about is refusal to take human life by warfare and murder and so."

Another opinion comes from Rev. J. Harold Kemmis a clergyman of the Church of England and a member of the Order of the Cross (London). He is reported to have spoken at Los Angeles as follows:

"Everybody wants peace, whether or not they are religious. But what kind of peace? When millions of lambs are about to be slaughtered, is that conducive to peace? If man really wants peace he must build all the condition which make for peace. Carnivorism is an evil force which helps war. It is for us to do something now which the United Nations is not doing, something which the churches could do but are not doing. Carnivorism is a barbarity - something evil - something hurtful - something which should bring a blush of shame to men, though many noble people have not perceived it thusly. Carnivorism is utterly wrong, vegetarianism is in line with Divine Law. Carnivorism is war on a certain level: it is war upon the less developed creatures of this planet. Carnivorism is a war in which the lesser creatures always lose. They have a right to life just as we humans do. Carnivorism encourages cruelty, it causes a group of people to make their living by abominable slaughtering. I believe carnivorism makes for war in that it encourages all those rough and beastial ways."

No one can deny the force of the above reasoning. As you sow, so shall you reap. Karmas work in their own way. One's actions are responsible for creating a good or bad character. In India a wise saying is *Jaisa Khave Anna, Waisa Hove Mana* — "As your diet, so your feelings."

More than a century ago, Brillat-Savarin, the French philosopher, also remarked:

"Tell me what you eat and I will tell you what you are!" It is certainly true, for food has an effect on character. *"Today the truth of this contention,"* writes the Editor of *"The Vegetarian News Digest"* *"is borne out by studies of human beings and by extensive research which show for instance, that whatever affects the endocrine glands deleteriously influences character and personality. These glands are influent in the whole process of digestion, as well as metabolism, and through the harmones produced from food they are directors of every activity of the body and mind."*

Dr. Louis Berman has analyzed the various traits in terms of diet and metabolism which establishes that man is made by what he eats and drinks. Jaina Tirthankaras knew this well and consequently they laid down ethical rules which regulate man's diet in an Ahimsaist manner. A Jain can never touch meat or fish or eggs and he can never drink intoxicants. The Jainas refuse meat on the following grounds:

"Flesh cannot be procured without causing destruction of life; one who uses flesh, therefore commits Himsa (Injury) unavoidably. If the flesh be that of a buffalo, ox, etc., which has died of itself, even then Himsa is caused by the crushing of creatures spontaneously born therein. Whether pieces of flesh are raw, or cooked, or in the process of cooking, spontaneously born creatures of the same genus are constantly being generated there. He who eats, or touches, a raw, or a cooked piece of flesh certainly kills a group of spontaneously born creatures gathering together.

In the whole world the Jainas are the only people who have never touched meat and wine since a hoary antiquity and yet they are well-off in all walks of life. They are most peaceful citizens and try to live out the Ahimsa principle so far as is possible for them.

Among the great teachers and other personages of the world, Zoroaster, Socrates, Pythagoras, Plato, Confucius, Christ, Muhammad, Plutarch, Ovid, Buddha, Mahavira, Nanak, Asoka, Pope, Tolstoy, Thoreaun, Walt Whitman, Shelley, M. Gandhi, R.L. Stevenson, John Ruskin, Sir Isaac Newton, Thomas Edison, Leonard da Vinci, Charles Darwin, George Bernard Shaw and others lived and preached Ahimsa. They knew well the intimate relationship between man and his food. Voltaire observed:

"Men who feed upon carnage and drink strong drinks have an impoisoned and acrid blood which drives them mad in a hundred different ways."

Ralph Waldo Trine, author of *"Every Living Creature"* declared:

"I share the belief with many others that the highest mental, physical and spiritual excellence will come to a person only when, among other things, he refrains from consuming flesh and blood."

The great Moghul Emperor of India, Akbar the Great, proclaimed:

"It is indeed from ignorance and cruelty that, although various kinds of food are obtainable, men are bent upon injuring living creatires, and lending a ready hand in killing and eating them; none seems to have an eye for the beauty inherent in the prevention of cruelty, but makes himself a tomb for animals."

(Ain-i-Akbari, by H. Blockmann, Vol. I p. 61)

Akbar was aware of the degenerating influence which the contact and company of flesh-mongers could create; hence he ordered that "butchers, fishermen and the like, who have no other occupation but taking life, should have a separate quarter and their asssociation with others should be prohibited by fine." (*Smith, Akbar, the Great Moghul,* pp. 335-336).

Christianity is plainly and emphatically against the killing of animals and declares that man's food is to be fruits and vegetables.

"Behold I have given you every herb bearing seed, which is upon the face of earth and every tree in which is the fruit of a tree yielding seed; to you it shall be for meat." — (Genesis 1: 29)

But today the nations of the West have forsaken the very spirit of Jesus Christ's sublime teaching and have forgotten the meaning of the Sermon on the Mount. In so doing they have lost the balance of mind, and with that the privilege of peaceful living. But in the East people are fortunate to have been blessed by the birth of a living Apostle of Ahimsa. Mahatma Gandhi was born in India to live a life of Ahimsa. His experiences in Truth are like a beaconlight to show the Right Path to an erring world. His opinion about the perfect food for men is remarkable. He wrote:

"I do not regard flesh food as necessary for us at any stage and under any clime in which it is possible for human beings ordinarily to live. I hold flesh food to be unsuited to our species. We err in copying the lower animal world, if we are superior to it. For one thing, the tremendous vested interests that have grown round the belief in animal food prevent the medical profession from approaching the question with complete detachment. Vegetarianism is one of the priceless gifts. It may not be lightly given up . . . . Abstention from meat is undoubtedly a great aid to the evolution of the spirit. Experience teaches that animal food is unsuited to those who would curb their passions. It is necessary to correct the error that vegetarianism has made us weak in mind or body or passive or inert in action. There is a great deal of truth in the saying that man becomes what he eats. The grosser the food the grosser the body. A man who wants to control his animal passions easily does so if he controls his palate."

Once when Mahatma Gandhi's second son, Manilal, had suffered seriously from a severe attack of typhoid, the medical doctor advised to give him eggs and chicken broth. The doctor warned Mahatmaji that his son's life was in danger and that this diet was necessary. In spite of this warning, Mahatmaji was quite serious and he thought that it is only on such occasions that a man's faith is truly tested. He wrote:

"Rightly or wrongly it is a part of my religious conviction that man may not eat meat, eggs and the like. There should be a limit even to the means of keeping ourselves alive. Even for life itself we may not do certain things. Religion, as I understand it, does not permit me to use meat or eggs for me or mine, even on occasions like this."

— (Autobiography, p. 180)

It is not only necessary to abjure from taking meat, fish and eggs on the ground of religious belief, but it is absolutely essential for a healthy and happy life. The medical opinion favours vegetarianism because that is the natural diet of human beings, as we have discussed and seen above. Some people think that there is no harm in taking eggs, but in this instance they commit a mistake because nature has provided eggs for procreation. They are not edibles and can not be the natural food of man. This is the reason that medical authorities like Dr. J. E. R. Modonagh condemned eggs and declared them harmful. To eat them is to commit the sin of infanticide.

Consequently, if the common man of the world wants to be happy, he should learn to control his lower nature and he should follow the human way of Ahimsa diet, as discussed above. The individual common man then and then alone will be able to awaken his inherent spiritual tendency. Then he will not eat for the pleasures of the palate but for the sake of health, which is to be acquired best by eating sun-baked fruits and vegetables. This change in diet will certainly change the heart of man, who then following his inner voice of Viveka, will turn out to be true in his efforts to live and work for Ahimsa. At this stage only, he can feel proud to be in a position to style and feel himself as a world citizen. The individual thus would be a safety and security to his own self and to others as well. Animals too, would be happy, for their ruthless massacre and slaughter will come to an end. Human beings, by sowing the seeds of Ahimsa, can naturally reap the blessed fruits of Ahimsa, which are joy, happiness and self-satisfaction. Then the land would yield and produce more grain, because the man could have earned the blessings of million of those saved animal souls. In this way only 'Grow more food' campaign would succeed and man would be happy in a world of plenty.

By the change in diet, man would be nearer to Ahimsa, because he would be able to alleviate in him the animal tendencies of lower nature which have become uppermost in his heart and are the root cause of conflict. Thus man would feel Oneness of Life; to him man and animal would be equal then. He will treat them as brethen and live with them in peaceful co-operation. Regions of abundance then will be alert and will vie with each other to ensure the basic needs of human beings all over the planet; for it is their duty in Ahimsa Law to render help and save their fellow beings.

With a changed heart, the vision will itself become clarified and the individual will feel pleasure in observing the vows of austerities in diet. Then common man will eat for the sake of health only and will deem it his duty to eat less, so that others may also have their shares and he may start the lesson to conquer the demon of hunger. Jains observe this vow, which they call "Unodara-Vrata". This mode of life saves food to a considerable quantity and causes no physical harm to the observer; rather it helps him to make progress in mutual co-operation and spiritiual advancement. It is, certainly, wrong to presume that in order to meet out the shortage of food grains in the world today, man should take to unnatural diet and eat fish and fowls. It would mean only to undermine the very foundation of Ahimsa belief and to push the common man in the dump of cruelty and barbarity, which will turn him to become more beastly in his daily dealings than ever before. The present crisis due to the shortage of food grain is the creation of man himself and he can easily ward it off provided he adheres to the principle of Ahimsa. Much of the tillable land today is utilised for growing tobacco crop and tons of edible grains are destroyed in producing alcohol. If man stops smoking and drinking intoxicants, which are a menace to mankind, the problem of the shortage of food would certainly be solved to a greater degree.

Besides, a greater area of tillable land is also left unsown as grazing ground for animals meant for provision of meat dishes. A modern agronomist has proved that an acre of land used for the grazing of cattle or sheep can produce about 1000 lbs. of animal food per annum, but the same acre can produce an average of 5000 lbs. of cereals, or as much as 20000 lbs. of vegetables such as potatoes, and probably some fruit in addition. With the world's population growing at such a pace that it will reach 10,000 million by the end of the century, as against 5,000 million today, the urgent necessity of using all land to the best possible advantage can readily be seen.

And when this economical vegetarian aspect will be substantiated with the sacred vow of observing austerities in diet, not only the crisis of food shortage will be removed, but man will contribute remarkably to create an atmosphere of universal peace and happiness. Richard B. Gregg, the renowned pacifist, is emphatic on the point, when he writes:

"I agree with the Jain belief that vegetarianism is now a real element in Ahimsa and a factor in the promotion of World Peace. There are now in this world too many people to be supported by the available acres of tillable land. Only if people stop eating meat can everyone be fed. So people who eat meat are causing others to starve."

Obviously the meat-eater is responsible for bringing about a deterioration and loss of cattle all over the world, which tells highly on the growth of grain production. Thus it is only Ahimsa which can solve all our problems, as well as can advance us in every respect.

An international Scientific Food Committee was set up after the first World War by the League of Nations, composed among others of representatives of Great Britain, U.S.A., Russia, France, Germany, Italy and Holland. The Honorable Mr. Peter Freeman, M.P. of Great Britain, informs that one of the questions this Committee was asked to answer was:

"What is the minimum meat ration necessary to keep a soldier on active service in good health?"

After securing expert military, medical and other evidence from all over the world Mr. Freemans answer, briefly, was:

"NONE — in view of the fact that perfect health can be maintained by a soldier on active service without any meat at all."

Thus it is obvious that meat is not necessary at all to sustain life. Most of the strongest and most enduring animals are vegetarians, including the horse, zebra, elephant, rhinoceros, buffalo, bison, all the deer tribe, giraffe, monkey, gorilla, cattle, sheep, and rabbits.

Many world records have been won by vegetarians of long standing and vegetarian workers have performed some of the greatest feats of strength and endurance.

In certain quarters, however, an objection is raised against vegetarian diet on the gound that the plants also have life; thus it also involves violence, i.e. 'Himsa,' to eat vegetables. But this objection is vain and thoughtless. No doubt, plants have life, but they are neither killed nor hurt in getting their products. When the fruits or the grain of wheat or barely are ripe, they become detached from the plants in their natural way. Nobody uproots a fruit or harvest tree in order to get its product; only a natural process is gone through to get them. But in meat diet, the animals are killed, rather butchered mercilessly for their flesh, which involves greater Himsa (injury) and creates a violent atmosphere. Moreover the Jain thinkers enlighten us in this respect. Every living being from the vegetable kingdom to man survive in life due to vitalities called 'PRANAS.' These Pranas (life vitalities) are ten in all, namely, the five senses of touch, taste, smell, sight and hearing, the three strengths of mind, speech, and body, and, finally, respiration and age. Man and animals possess all the ten vitalities, while vegetable life has only four. In vegetable life these four vitalities are the sense of touch, strength of body, respiration and age. Now if there could be any tinge of violence in procuring a vegetarian diet then it is of the lowest and least degree. The motive behind the vegetarian diet is to cause not even the least possible injury to life. Certainly a vegetarian does not want to hurt even the vegetable life. He satisfies his hunger with the products of plants such as fruits, nuts, dry grains, etc., which nature provides itself. In fact, a vegetarian life creates a peaceful and prosperous atmosphere, which is most beneficial for humanity at large.

This is the way of Ahimsa life, which a true Jaina layman lives gladly. The Jaina tradition abounds with many humane deeds of its enthusiastic followers of Ahimsa.

Thus the real solution of the food problem of the world today is hidden in food reform and in the adoption of a life of Ahimsa. Through Ahimsa the food craving instinct of man can be regulated and controlled. Being vegetarians and Ahimsaists at the same time, mankind can become self-sufficient and satisfied.

VEGETARIANISM and RELIGIONS OF THE WORLD

CHAPTER IV
VEGETARIANISM and RELIGIONS OF THE WORLD

In chapter three we have demonstrated that for a healthy and spiritual life it is important to be a vegetarian, which is one of the fundamental principles of Jainism. From time immemorial Jain sages have taught that no one has the right to take the life of others. This is the principle of "live and let live". Now let us examine what saints, prophets and reformers in all ages have said about vegetarianism.

HINDUISM—

RIGVEDA —

1. O Fire! devour the meat-eaters. (10/87/2)

2. O Mitra! break the head of those who eat the flesh of animals. (10/87/16)

ATHARVAVEDA —

1. I destroy those who eat flesh and eggs. (8/6/13)

MAHABHARATA —

1. No recitation of the Vedas, no performance of yajnas, no homage to holy places, or no bathing in holy waters, can equal the merit earned by being kind to animals. (Shanti-parva)

2. Those who eat despicable objects like animal flesh, etc., in place of various kinds of vegetable food full of nectar, are, in sooth, demons. (Anushasana-p.)

3. He who wishes to grow his own flesh by adding to it flesh of other living beings is the most cruel and mean person. (-ibid.)

MANU'S CODE —

1. All those who kill living beings, advise others to kill them, cut into pieces the bodies of killed animals, sell meat, purchase it, cook it, serve it and eat it are sinners and wicked.

   The flesh of the animal I eat in this life, that animal shall without doubt eat mine in my next birth. (5/55)

2. Flesh cannot be obtained without killing beasts. Killing of animals does not lead to heaven, hence one must renounce eating

flesh. Considering the origin of flesh, which is a kind of transformed menstrual blood, and the pangs of death and incarceration the beasts suffers, one must forswear eating flesh of all kinds. (5/48-49)

JAINISM —

Life is dear to all. Every living being desires to live happily its span of life. Therefore, hurt no living being.

Let no one injure life, but be as assiduous in cherishing the life of other beings as one's own, for Ahimsa (non-injury) is the highest religion.

BUDDHISM —

1. Flesh is foul smelling. The Mlechchhas eat it. The Arya (good) people do not touch it. An Arya does not take flesh and blood because these are inedible and despicable.

   Meat-eating destroys sainthood or Brahmanahood. A meat-eater is a robber who deprives others of their life forces forcibly.

   Those who, out of greed, kill other living beings, or finance the production of meat are sinners and wicked and become denizens of hell to suffer unaccountable misery for their misdeeds.

   I believe that he who eats the flesh of others, in fact, eats the flesh of his own son.

   Meat-eating results in nasty and dangerous diseases like leprosy; the body becomes the abode of dangerous germs. Hence, give up meat-eating.

   In no Sutra have I upheld meat-eating, nor permitted meat-eating, nor declared it to be good food.

   O wise one! I have already given instruction that food approved by saints should consist of rice, barley, wheat, pulses, ghee, oil, milk, sugar, etc. (Lankavatara Sutra, ch. 8)

2. Even as a mother watcheth over her child, her only child, as long as life doth last, so let us, for all creatures, great or small, develop such a boundless heart and mind. Ay, let us practise love for all the world, upward and downward, yonder thence uncramped, free from ill-will and enmity.

(— Sutta Nipata)

CHANAKYA-NITI —

The meat-eaters, the drinkers of spirits, the illiterate, and the ignoramous are like animals (beasts); mother earth always suffers on account of them.

ZOROASTRIANISM —

The wicked man, who unlawfully made much slaughter of cattle and sheep and other quadrupeds, has his own limbs broken and separated. (— Arda Viraf, 174-192)

The souls of the wicked man and woman who killed the other in the water and smote and slew other creatures of Ahura Mazda (God), had to eat excreta. (— Arda Viraf, 201)

Ahura Mazda (God) considers kindness to animals the best religion.

JUDAISM —

"And God said, 'Behold, I have given you every plant yielding seed which is upon the face of all the earth, and every tree with seed in its fruit; you shall have them for food. And to every beast of the earth, and to every bird of the air, and to everything that creeps on the earth, everything that has the breath of life, I have given every green plant for food."   Genesis 1:29-30

ALBIGENSIANISM —

You will make this commitment to God; that you will never, knowingly or of your own will, eat flesh of birds, or creeping things, or of animals, prohibited by the Church of God.

CHRISTIANITY —

'Thou shalt not kill' (Ten Commandments)
'Blessed are they who eat the kindly fruits of the earth' (St. Luke)
'God wishes that we shall not hurt our humble brethren (animals), but should help them whenever they require it.' (St. Francis of Assisi)

Let us not therefore judge one another any more: but judge this rather, that no man put a stumblingblock or an occasion to fall in his brother's way. I know, and am persuaded by the Lord Jesus, that there is nothing unclean of itself but to him that esteemeth any thing to be unclean, to him it is unclean. But if thy brother be grieved with thy meat, now walkest though not charitably. Destroy not him with thy meat, for whom Christ died . . . .

For meat destroy not the work of God. All things indeed are pure; but it is evil for that man who eateth with offence. It is good neither to eat flesh, nor to drink wine, nor any thing whereby thy brother stumbleth, or is offended, or is made weak.
(St. Paul, Romans 14:13-15, 20-21)

ISLAM

"There is not an animal on the earth, nor a flying creature flying on two wings, but they are peoples like unto you." — Koran, *surah* 6, verse 38

"Therewith He causes crops to grow for you, and the olive and the date-palm and grapes and all kinds of fruit. Lo! Herein is indeed a portent for people who reflect." — Koran, *surah* 16, verse 11

" . . . but to hunt . . . is forbidden you, so long as ye are on the pilgrimage. Be mindful of your duty to Allah, unto Whom you will all be gathered." — Koran, *surah* 5, verse 96

"A token unto them is the dead earth. We revive it, and We bring forth from it grain — so that they will eat thereof. As We have placed therein gardens of the date-palm and grapes, and We have caused springs of water to gush forth therein. That they may eat of the fruit thereof, and their hands created it not. Will they not, then, give thanks?" — Koran, *surah* 36, verses 33-35

"Maim not the brute beasts." — Prophet Mohammed

"Whoever is kind to the lesser creatures is kind to himself" — Prophet Mohammed

All creatures are members of the one family of God. — Koran

SIKHISM —

He who eats flesh and drinks intoxicants destroys merit in the whole.

SWAMI DAYANAND (Arya Samaj) —

There is no mention of meat-eating in the Vedas; even to eat out of the hands of a meat-eater and drunkard makes one guilty of meat-eating. O' meat-eaters, when after a time no animals will be left, will you stoop to eating human flesh?

We should feel detached from worldly objects. Jain thinkers have said, "Live in the world like a lily in a tank." A person blessed with this view adopts a pure and pious life of his own accord. Vincent Smith in his *History of India*, remarks, "Jain ethics are meant for men of all positions, for kings, warriors, traders, artisans, agriculturists and indeed for men and women in every walk of life. Do your duty and do it as humanely as you can. This in brief is the primary principle of Jainism."

In this age we should have a cosmopolitan outlook and we should treat all life as sacred. This humane outlook heralds an era of peace, plenty and prosperity. It is therefore apt to conclude that only the religion of peace and rational outlook will be able to establish individual as well as universal peace. In order that our mental vision may remain bright and clear we should ever remember these sublime words of Acharya Amitgati.

"O my lord, make myself such that I may always have love for all living beings, pleasure in the company of the virtuous, sympathy for the afflicted and tolerance for those perversely inclined."

May peace and contentment bless the world.

VEGETARIANISM AND MORAL THINKERS

CHAPTER V
VEGETARIANISM
and
MORAL THINKERS

Jain masters have ordained that intentional injury to the living must be abandoned at any cost. We must not forget that all of a sudden our bulb of life will get fused. It is therefore advisable that we should treat others as brothers and friends. The soul which is over-brimming with the nectar of fellow-feeling and universal brotherhood is the object of universal veneration. Pure mind is the abode of Godhood. Now let us examine what famous moral thinkers have to say about vegetarianism.

- 1 -

I fully believe that vegetarianism can offer humanity a solid foundation for internal and external peace. World peace or any other kind of peace depends greatly on the attitude of the mind. Vegetarianism can bring about the right mental attitude for peace. In this world of lusts and hatreds, greed and anger, force and violence vegetarianism holds forth a way of life, which if practised universally can lead to a better, juster and more peaceful community of nations.

—U. Nu, Prime Minister of Burma

- 2 -

Beware, O mortals, of defiling your bodies with sinful food. There are fruits bending their branches down by their weight, and luxurious grapes on the vines. There are sweet vegetables and herbs which the flame can render palatable and mellow. Nor are you denied milk, nor honey, fragrance of the aroma of the thyme flower. The bountiful earth offers you an abundance of pure food and provides for meals obtainable without slaughter and bloodshed.

—Pythagoras, Greek Philosopher (582?-500? B.C.E.)

- 3 -

All ancient philosophy was based on plain living. In this sense the few vegetarian philosophers have contributed more for the welfare of man than all the other philosophers together.

—Friedrich Nietzsche

- 4 -

The natural Law cannot be changed from time to time. A good act bears a good fruit and an evil act bears bad fruit. That is called the Law of Karma. To that order of the natural

Law of Karma belongs the law that the destruction of life brings an evil effect on the doer. Hence do not eat meat and eggs, which cause destruction of life.

—Dr. W.J. Jayasurya

- 5 -

The wrong custom of flesh-eating is detrimental to man's physical, mental, and spiritual welfare, whereas vegetarian food is favourable to purity, to charity and to perfect control of the appetites and passions.

—Dr. Crambell Booth

- 6 -

To affirm life is to deepen, to make more inward, and to exalt the will-to-live.

At the same time the man who has become a thinking being feels a compulsion to give to every will-to-live the same reverence for life that he gives to his own. He experiences that other life as his own. He accepts as being good: to preserve life, to raise to its highest value life which is capable of development; and as being evil; to destroy life, to injure life, to repress life which is capable of development. This is the absolute, fundamental principle of the moral, and it is a necessity of thought.

—Albert Schweitzer (1875-1965)

- 7 -

There is nothing that revolts our moral sense so much as cruelty. Every other offence we can pardon, but not cruelty. The reason is found in the fact that cruelty is the exact opposite of compassion whereon, in the last resort, all satisfaction and all well-being and happiness depend. It is this compassion alone which is the real basis of all voluntary justice and genuine loving kindness. It is asserted that beasts have no rights; the illusion is harboured that our conduct, so far as they are concerned, has no moral significance or that there are no duties to be fulfilled towards animals. Such a view is one of revolting coarseness — a barbarism of the West. Compassion for animals is intimately connected with goodness of character, and it may be confidently asserted that he who is cruel to living creatures cannot be a good man.

—Schopenhauer

- 8 -

The hunter and butcher are not symbols of spirituality. They are not embodiments of the higher mental and social powers of man's nature.

—Herbert M. Sheltoy

- 9 -

Wild animals never kill for sport. Man is the only one to whom the torture to death of his fellow creatures is amusing in itself.

—James Anthony Froude

- 10 -

Animals are dumb and therefore they cannot adequately express their pain or suffering. It is the duty of man not only to show sympathy and compassion to animals but also to treat them as his equals.

—R. Krishnan

- 11 -

Cruelty to animals is not only a stupid act, but it is an insult to God.

—Sir Isaac Newton (1643-1727)
Scientist and Mathmetician

- 12 -

As soon as one knows the truth contained in vegetarianism and continues to eat meat he is no more innocent and ignorant of his mistake. He is guilty of crime.

—Benzion Liber

- 13 -

My stomach is not a graveyard for dead animals.

—George Bernard Shaw (1856-1950)

- 14 -

I believe that the tendency is towards vegetarian diet, that it will be recognized as fit and proper, and that the time is not far distant when the idea of animal food will be revolting to the civilized man.

—Sir Edward Saunders

- 15 -

The longest livers, such as Thomas Parr and Madame Prieux and others who lived for about 150 years on this planet, were all vegetarians.

—Mr. Nibcomb

- 16 -

I have abstained from flesh, fish and fowl for 62 years, and I have been observant of the rules of health. I have never had a headache, never been in bed a whole day from illness, or suffered pain except from trivial accidents. I have had a very happy and, I hope, a somewhat useful life; and now in my 88th year I am as light as a blossom and as capable of receiving a new idea as I was 20 years ago.

—Mr. Samuel Saunders

One of the first things my dear teacher (Barrister C. R. Jain) asked of me was to stop eating flesh food, which I did at once, as did my husband also. We have gone without any kind of meat in our diet since then (1933), and our continued health and freedom from pain and disease of any kind and the difference in our feelings, generally, is all the proof we need of the wisdom of abstaining from all meat in the diet. If any one would just stop eating meat, all kinds including fish and fowl, for just one year and see the difference in the feeling, in the health, in the keenness of intellect and in the general feelings of cleanliness, they would not go back to it.

—Mrs. Evelyn S. Kleinschmidt, USA

- 19 -

Complete non-violence is complete absence of ill-will against all that lives. It therefore embraces even sub-human life, not excluding noxious insects and beasts. They have not been created to feed our destructive propensities. If we only knew the mind of the Creator, we should find their proper place in His creation.

—Mahatma Gandhi (1869-1948)

- 20 -

Truly man is the king of beasts, for his brutality exceeds them. We live by the death of others. We are burial places! I have since an early age abjured the use of meat . . .

—Leonardo da Vinci (1452-1519)

- 21 -

When a man wants to murder a tiger, he calls it sport; when a tiger wants to murder him, he calls it ferocity.

—George Bernard Shaw (1856-1950)

- 22 -

I still believe that man not having been given the power of creation does not possess the right of destroying the meanest creature that lives. The prerogative of destruction belongs soley to the creator of all that lives.

—Mahatma Gandhi (1869-1948)

- 23 -

We are the living graves of murdered beasts,
Slaughtered to satisfy our appetites
We never pause to wonder at our feats
If kine, like men, can possibly have rights.

We pray on Sundays that we may have light,
To guide our footsteps on the path we tread.

We're sick of war, do not not want to fight
The thought of it now fills our hearts with dread
And yet — we gorge ourselves upon the dead.

Like carrion crows, we live and feed on meat
Regardless of the suffering and pain
We cause by doing so, if thus we treat
Defenceless animals for sport or gain,
How can we hope in this world to attain
The peace we say we are so anxious for.

We pray for it, o'er the tombs of slain
To God, while outraging the moral law
Thus cruelty begets its offspring War.

—George Bernard Shaw (1856-1950)

- 24 -

I do feel that spiritual progress does demand at some stage that we should cease to kill our fellow creatures for the satisfaction of our bodily wants.

It ill becomes us to invoke in our daily prayers the blessings of God, the compassionate, if we in turn will not practice elementary compassion towards our fellow creatures.

—Mahatma Gandhi (1869-1948)

- 25 -

What gives man the right to kill an animal, often torture it, so that he can fill his belly with its flesh?

I personally believe that as long as human beings will go on shedding the blood of animals, there will never by any peace

We are obliged not to take life — we should not take the attitude that we are doing the animals a favor by not eating them. They have a right to live just as much as we have a right to live.

People often say that humans have always eaten animals as if this is a justification for continuing this practice. According to this logic we should not try to prevent people from murdering other people since this has also been done since the earliest of times.

—Isaac Bashevis Singer, Nobel Laureate

- 26 -

Meat eaters are 'burial places' that their bodies become graveyards for the animals they devour.

The time will come when men will look on the murder of animals as they now look on the murder of men.

For the benefit of your gullet you have made of yourself a grave for all animals.

—Leonardo da Vinci (1452-1519)

Those who abstain from flesh foods will experience a greater spiritual consciousness — the eye of the soul will become free, and will be established as in a port beyond the smoke and the waves of the corporeal nature.

—Porphyry (232?-304?)

- 28 -

Flesh eating is simply immoral, it involves the performance of an act which is contrary to moral feeling — killing. Vegetarianism is, nonetheless, an issue of particular importance because it is a sign that the aspiration of mankind towards moral perfection is serious and sincere, for it has taken the one unalterable order of succession natural to it, beginning with the first step.

—Leo Tolstoy (1828-1910)

- 29 -

I do not see any reason why animals should be slaughtered to serve as human diet when there are so many substitutes. After all, man can live without meat . . .

—The Dalai Lama

- 30 -

As long as men massacre animals, they will kill each other. Indeed, he who sows the seeds of murder and pain cannot reap joy and love.

—Pythagoras, Greek Philosopher
(582?-500? B.C.E.)

- 31 -

Educate the children in their infancy in such a way that they become exceedingly kind and merciful to the animals.

—Abdul Baha, Baháí

Ahimsa, the doctrine of non-violence is the supermost weapon in the arsenal of the pious souls. We should also bear this truth in mind that the first seed of true philosophy is there, where we see the sprout of respect for the life of other beings. How can you call a man philosopher, in other words a wise man, who destroys life and thus digs his own grave by debasing inhuman propensities? Wisdom is there where one regards others as his fellow creatures. The life based upon torture of living beings is not really cultured. Virtually it is the culture of vultures.

Lust, luxury and licentiousness are constantly dragging our mind to satisfy the animal passions. It needs superior mental training to control animal cravings gradually by constant and sincere efforts as explained by the Masters — the Tirthankaras. We can thus advance on the path of the moral plane.

We should also bear in mind that the life of violence cannot confer real joy. It is powerless and leads to darkness, but the life of Ahimsa blesses the soul with delight, might and light. Ahimsa must lead to life, light and immortality. This Ahimsa is the essence of religions. Therefore we should try our best to practice the religion of compassion and love and achieve everlasting peace.

Let us all with courage, conviction and sincerity proceed towards the divine path of purity, piety, peace and perennial joy and attain Nirvana — the ultimate aim of every aspirant.

VEGETARIANISM and MEDICAL SCIENTISTS

CHAPTER VI
VEGETARIANISM AND MEDICAL SCIENTISTS

Vegetarianism

"Vegetable," once rated as a contemptuous epithet generally pressed into service to describe an inert person, has staged a comeback in the West as a vibrant, lifegiving product. Vegetarians are no longer regarded as freaks or faddists. Even on Harley Street of London, food specialists now recommend a balanced vegetarian diet for all those who want to avoid coronary or cancer. The legend goes that it was George Bernard Shaw who struck a mighty blow for vegetables and vegetarians. Interrogated by a bunch of inquisitive pressmen about the secret of his phenomenal success, he said with a straight face: "First I studied my father and his way of life for he was a miserable failure. I found out that he was a strict non-vegetarian, a chain-smoker and a drunkard, so I decided to be a vegetarian and a teetotaller. Now you can publish it as my success story."

It might be observed that the comsumption of meat is not a prerequisite either for physical or intellectual vigour, strength or energy. The fact that the strongest of animals — the elephant, the bison and hippopotamus, the fastest of animals — the horse and the deer, thrive exclusively on a vegetable diet, and that many of the profoundest thinkers and philosophers of the world, both in the East and in the West, have also been abstainers from meat may be cited as relevant illustrations.

Vegetarian athletes, ranging from Greek marathon runners to modern swimmers, weight-lifters, wrestlers, and long distance runners and cyclists have demonstrated that the peak of physical fitness can be achieved without slaughter-house products.

Whoever hides behind it, and sometimes we vegetarians do — the health argument is a spurious one. Some vegetarians are strong, some weak, as are meat-eaters also. Some live long, some die prematurely. It is the reverence for life of one's way which distinguishes it from the others and the common denomination is what is called vegetarianism.

After realizing all the facts and covering the broad aspects of vegetarianism, let it not be said that without meat a man cannot sustain a healthy body, mind and spirit.

Meat is absolutely unnecessary for perfectly healthy existence, and the best work can be done on a vegetarian diet.

—Prof. Woodhead, M.D., F.R.C.P., F.R.S.

- 2 -

Today there is the scientific fact assured that man belongs not to the flesh-eaters but to the fruit-eaters. Today there is the chemical fact in the hands of all, which none can gainsay, that the products of the vegetable kingdom contain all that is necessary for the fullest sustenance of human life. Flesh is an unnatural food, and, therefore, tends to create functional disturbance. As it is taken in modern civilization, it is infected with such terrible diseases readily communicable to men as cancer, consumption, fever, intestinal worms, etc., to an enormous extent. There is little need to wonder that flesh-eating is one of the most serious causes of the diseases that carry off ninety-nine out of every hundred people that are born.

—Dr. Josia Oldfield

- 3 -

It is a vulgar error to regard meat in any form as necessary to life. All that is necessary to the human body can be supplied by the vegetable kingdom. . . . The vegetarian can extract from his food all the principles necessary for the growth and support of the body, as well as for the production of heat and force. It must be admitted as a fact beyond all questions that some persons are stronger and more healthy who live on that food. I know how much of the prevailing meat diet is not mearly a wasteful extravagance but a source of serious evil to the consumer. The meat diet is a source of several incurable diseases, e.g., cancer, arthritis, heart disease, scorfula, etc.

—Sir Henry Thompson, F.R.C.S.

- 4 -

Economically speaking, flesh is not necessary; and meat seriously diseased may be so prepared as to look fairly good. Many an animal with advanced disease of the lung shows to the naked eye no appearance in the flesh which differs from the normal.

—A. Winter Blyth, F.R.C.S.

- 5 -

It is interesting to note that scientific men all over the world are awakening to the fact that the flesh of animals as food is not a pure nutriment, but is mixed with poisonous substances, excrementitious in character, which are the natural results of animal life. The vegetable stores up energy. It is from the vegetable world that all animals directly or indirectly derive the energy which is manifested by the animal life through muscular and mental work. The vegetable builds up energy; the animal spends energy.

—Dr. H. J. Kellogg

No great eater of flesh ever lived to be a centenarian. Why? Because the flesh-eater makes his heart beat 20,000 times a day more than a non-flesh-eater.

—Dr. J. Henry

Reason tells us specifically that fruits, nuts and vegetables plus plain water is the diet for the normal human being. Vegetables and fruits have their own salts and savour; they are complete foods in themselves and require no disguise except for perverted appetites. They are, too, less gross than flesh foods and the body which receives them becomes more refined and the offence to the soul less severe — this is the path to true happiness. Moreover, most animals when violently killed, die in abject fear; fear causes a radical chemical change in an animal body and the flesh becomes thereby highly acid . . . only the depraved or ignorant human beings eat it.

—Dr. William Henry Talbot

The diseases of the liver, kidneys and all other internal organs are mostly cured by vegetarian diet.

—Dr. Neiscence

Animal meat may directly engender many painful and loathsome diseases. Scorfula itself, the fecund source of suffering and death, not improbably owes its origin to flesh-eating habits.

—Dr. A. Kingford, Paris University

In order to produce veal meat the physiology of the calf is disturbed. When you get the meat, you are not eating from what I would call a healthy animal. So I just don't think we want to be a part of that scene. Also, there are a large number of drugs that are given to farm animals and a lot of these drugs have residues that remain in the meat, and give another component in the diet that I don't wish to have any part of.

—Dr. Ross Hall
Biochemist & Professor
McMaster University, Canada

When eggs are eaten in great amounts the cholesterol content of the blood rises and the tendency towards the development of gallstones, hardening of tissues and perhaps other diseases increases. Eggs are also said to be a prominent cause of Bright's disease and other forms of kidney impairment.

—Drs. Irving Davidson and Robert Gross

Eggs are acid-forming, having an excess of nitrogen, fat and phospheric acid and cannot therefore form the natural diet of man.

—Dr. Govind Raj

Eggs are harmful. The serum or white of the egg is purely albumen. The body eliminates albumen as a cellular waste. The yoke of the egg contains cholesterol, a waxy alcohol which deposits in the liver and blood vessels, producing corrosion and hardening of the arteries.

—Dr. J. Amon-Wilkins

Eggs are deficient in calcium and do not contain carbohydrates. So their tendency is to favour putrefactive decomposition in the intestines rather than to encourage fermentative organisms to develop . . . . Consumption of meat and eggs lead to the generation of toxic substances which induce lethargy.

—Dr. E. V. McCollum

15

Eggs in many people are a potent factor in rendering the mutation forms of the bacillus coli communis pathogenic and this is doubtless due to the intensive egg-laying to which hens are being subjected. The rising incidence of disease is largely the result of the intensive farming methods which are employed today.

—Dr. J.E.R. McDonagh

In this age of science practically all the minerals and the vitamins can be supplied artifically and these could supplement milk where necessary. Dependence on meat and eggs for proteins, minerals and vitamins is no longer necessary. I feel confident that a vegetarian diet properly constructed is as nourishing as a diet containing meat and eggs.

—Dr. Ananda Nirmalasuria

17

After being well informed, few people would like to continue the consumption of eggs, not only for the cruelty to these poor exploited animals (hens, etc.), but also for their own health. Eggs are too high in cholesterol, one important cause of arteries, heart, brain and kidney diseases and gallstones. Fruits and vegetables and vegetable oils have none or hardly any cholesterol.

—Dr. Katherine Nimmo

Vegetarians less prone to chronic diseases —

Dr. Gordon Latto, President, International Vegetarian Union, has done some research into the medical aspects of vegetarianism and has arrived at some miraculous results.

All doctors agree that the right type of food plays a very important part in the cure of diseases, and serves as a means of maintaining and protecting health.

Vegetarians are better protected against some chronic diseases than the meat-eaters, researchers in Britain and the United States show.

The incidence of heart diseases and some forms of cancer is strikingly low among vegetarians.

Writing in 'New Scientist', Dr. Alan Long, a chemist in the research section of Britain's Vegetarian Society, says that much of the prejudice against vegetarian diet was based on the belief that plant food alone provided too little protein.

But experiments in dietary research in the past 20 years have conclusively proved that conditions of malnutrition that once were ascribed exclusively to lack of protein are actually caused by lack of food in general — of energy, as well as of protein.

Specific signs of protein deficiency are not evident in vegetarians and combinations of pulses and grains abetted by potato are now considered to be adequate sources of protein.

Explaining the low incidence of heart diseases among vegetarians, Dr. Long says that there are two main categories of fat in the diet, the triglycerides and cholesterol. Both these classes of fat are found in the blood. A high intake of triglycerides can raise blood cholesterol levels.

Triglycerides are of two kinds, saturated and unsaturated. Whereas the saturated fats do indeed raise blood cholesterol levels, unsaturated fats reduce blood cholesterol levels.

In general the fats of animals are highly saturated while the oils of plants tend to be unsaturated with a few notable exceptions like coconut oil and palm oil.

All evidence suggests that vegetarians should be less likely to suffer from heart attacks and strokes.

The best proof of this came from a study done recently in California on vegetarian and non-vegetarian Seventh Day Adventists, who do not smoke or drink.

The study found that non-vegetarian men between 35 and 64 were three times as likely to die of coronary heart disease as vegetarian men of the same age.

The lower incidence of cancer among vegetarians has been ascribed to higher intake of fibre.

Fibre clearly reduces the time the food takes to pass from mouth to anus. The long transmit times resulting from low fibre diets of non-vegetarians allow toxins produced by bacteria in the gut to remain in contact with the gut wall for longer, giving rise to diverticular disease as well as cancer of the large intestine and rectum and a whole host of other problems.

The faeces of omnivorous subjects contain higher concentrations of bile acids than do those of vegetarians and they also contain higher numbers of the bacteroid species of bacteria which can convert bile acids into carcinogenic bile salts.

In addition to bowel cancers, various studies suggest that high-fat, low fibre diets may contribute to cancer of the pancreas, breast, ovary, prostate and womb.

Vegetarians have lesser risk of food poisoning than non-vegetarians. Four out of five cases of food poisoning in Britain are traced to meat and its products.

Altogether the signs are that, contrary to some expectations, vegetarians are more healthy than meat-eating omnivores.

Dental cavities are very prevalent among those who eat refined foods, especially sugar. When dental cavities are treated by a vegetarian diet the process of falling teeth is arrested and loose teeth become firm again. Diseases such as Beri-Beri have been successfully treated by vegetarian foods with a high vitamin B content found in unpolished rice. Scurvy has been treated successfully by giving the patient vitamin C which is normally found in raw fruits and vegetables.

Constipation, which is usually associated with a non-vegetarian diet rich in refined food like white flour and white sugar, and food rich in animal protein, can be cured by having adequate raw food rich in roughage in the diet. Colitis or gastric or internal ulcers, caused by cooked or non-vegetarian diet can also be cured by having adequate raw food in the diet.

Chronic rheumatism in knees can be cured by a diet rich in fresh vegetable foods and having a minimum of protein and calories.

Blood pressure, causing heart disease and cerebral haemorrhage, the most killing disease in the world today after cancer, has often been cured by adopting a vegetarian balanced food reform diet.

The fact that a vegetarian balanced diet is far superior to the ordinary meat diet has been proved conclusively by hundreds of leading physiologists of the world.

CONCLUSION

CHAPTER 7
CONCLUSION

There was a time when, due largely to ignorance and apathy, certain wrong notions, misunderstandings and erroneous presumptions had become current, even in the circles of the supposedly well-informed, regarding the genesis, antiquity, nature, scope and significance of the Jaina system of religion, thought and culture. Thanks to the patient studies and laborious investigations of a horde of learned Indologists, Western and Indian, the fog of ignorance and unwarranted prejudice has been considerably dispelled. It is now no more necessary to prove that Jainism is an absolutely independent, highly developed, very comprehensive and ancient system, not unreasonably described as 'the oldest living religion', or 'the earliest home religion of India.' It is, indeed, found to have been in existence, in one form or the other, or under one name or the other, since the very dawn of human civilization, continuing without break throughout the pre-historical (pre-written historical), proto-historical and historical times.

The late Dr. Heinrich Zimmer, who is reputed to have been the greatest German Indologist of modern times, in his celebrated posthumous work, *The Philospohies of India,* conceded that there is truth in the Jaina idea that their religion goes back to a remote antiquity, the antiquity in question being that of the pre-Āryan, so-called Dravidian period, and that Jainism is the oldest of all Dravidian-born philosophies and religions. He also psychologically demonstrated that Jaina Yoga originated in pre-Āryan India, and has nothing to do with orthodox Brāhmanism which simply appropriated it in later centuries. Noel Retting, another Indologist, writes, "Only in Jainism, of all the living religions, do we see a fusion of the primitive with the profound. It has preserved elements from that first stage of man's religious awareness, animism. It affirms the separateness of spirit from matter, even though our modern philosophers and religionists regard any form of dualism as untenable. Despite the opinion of these men, Jainism is fundamentally scientific. And, it may very well be, contrary to the opinions of many anthropologists and students of comparative religion, the oldest living faith." And, Professor L. P. Tessitori is of opinion that "Jainism is of a very high order. Its important teachings are based upon science. The more the scientific knowledge advanced the more the Jaina teachings will be proved."

In fact, the Jaina system of thought is so wonderfully consistent with modern realism and science that one may easily be tempted to question its antiquity, about which, however, there is now no doubt.

Moreover, as Dr. Walthur Schubring observes, "He who has a thorough knowledge of the structure of the world cannot but admire the inward logic and harmony of Jain ideas. Hand in hand with the refined cosmographical ideas goes a high standard of astronomy and mathematics." Dr. Hermann Jacobi also believes that "Jainism goes back to a very early period, and to primitive currents of religious and metaphysical speculation which gave rise to the oldest Indian philosophies. They (the Jains) seem to have worked out their system from the most primitive notions about matter."

One of the fundamental as well as primitive ideas on which Jaina metaphysics is based is often described as animism. Jainism believes that not only all human beings and all the animals, but also all insects, all vegetation, even earth, stones, water, fire and air are living organisms, are all endowed with their respective souls, and, therefore, represent embodied life in various forms. This animistic belief is the chief source of respect for life, for all forms of living beings, however lowly, small or insignificant, proving at the same time that 'ahimsā' (non-injury to life), which is the very keynote of Jainism, is not only the greatest conception, but also one of the most ancient in the world. As the late Dr. Rajendra Prasad, the first President of free India, observed, "Jainism has contributed to the world the sublime doctrine of Ahimsā. No other religion has emphasised the importance of Ahimsā and carried its practice to the extent that Jainism has done". To quote yet another scholar, Mrs. Elizabeth Sharpe, "The Jaina philosophy is an almost perfect one. It is a live philosophy, ennobling and reassuring. It puts a supreme and beautiful value on life, believing that when its fragments are disintegrated to a point almost of nothingness, there is danger to that small evolution losing itself. This philosophy gives a sanctity to life and its preservation. This sanctity of life, it insists, is the highest religion, the only evolution. This philosophy is optimistic; for it believes, too, that in the end, right, that is life, soul, spirit, must triumph over matter; for once consciousness is restored to life in the form of 'right knowledge', matter has no longer any power over the soul." It is no doubt true that no other philosophy ever tried to carry the antithesis between spirit and matter so much to its logical conclusion as the Jaina. It, and therefore its followers, the Jains, consistently upheld the superiority of the soul over the body, and sacrificed the latter at the alter of the former. In this conception lies the secret of the success which Jainism has achieved in moulding the lives of countless people to a higher plane of mental discipline, purity of thought, and spiritual evolution. It is a way of life which is fully capable of raising an ordinary individual to the highest height of spiritual realization as preached by and embodied in the lives of Tirthankaras like Ṛṣabha, Aristanemi, Pārśva and

Mahāvīra. It is a system which offers much that is permanent and eternal, and has stood the test of time. It has helped and can still help humanity to regain its inner balance, which is the crying need of the present age. There is without doubt great ethical value in Jainism for man's improvement.

Every human being, nay every living being, is a soul, though an embodied and mundane one, hence an imperfect one, but one which is, in its essence, pure, immortal, eternal and blissful. Every man and woman and child, however strong or weak, high or low, without respect of race, caste or birth, has that divine spark, the infinite, omnipotent and omniscient soul in him or her, which is waiting only to be realized. One has but to arise, awake and free himself from the hypnotism of weakness, from ignorance and delusion, assert oneself and proclaim the God within him. He has to realize that he is not matter, is not a body, but a spirit free which is not a slave of matter, rather it can make matter its most obedient servant. With this realization of the self, of its infinite possiblity and capacity to become great and good, the aspirant launches on a course of self-discipline and self-purification. His sincere efforts at once being to bear fruit and ultimately enable him to attain liberation which means freedom — absolute freedom from the bondage of good as well as from the bondage of evil, because a golden chain is as much a chain as an iron one.

What is needed is a clear intellectual perception of the essential nature, present condition and potentialities of the self, and an unflinching conviction and faith in it, together with a persistent, practical pursuit of the goal in our daily life, which and which alone can keep us true to the centre of Truth. Obviously, imperfection, which means the present conditions of the mundane existence, is only tolerated because and so long as we do not get rid of it. Therefore, all worldly endeavour, being the child of the living soul's union with non-living matter, is to be tolerated only to be renounced ultimately. Until, for practical reasons, that stage of total renunciation and detachment arrives, the imperfect state, the worldly life as it is, has to be tolerated and controlled and regulated so as to keep it within the limits of the most minimum harm to Perfection, the essential nature of the Self. Of course, you may live your life, and live it with a zest, unfolding your personality to the fullest stature, bringing out the best in you, and putting in your utmost efforts for making life a success in every possible respect, for your own good and for the good of others. Everyone must strive to become a good citizen of the world, a humane civilized and cultured individual who values cooperation and co-existence, peace and happiness, and believes in universal brotherhood. For the common run of men and women, Jainism advocates a course of life which consists in a happy blending of the three living activities, Dharma, Artha and Kāma, and which tends to make a person a good, noble, gentle, happy and successsful citizen of the world.

Jainism took its firm roots in a peaceful civilization, not in a power civilization, hence it provided maximum liberty and tolerance. It is a very practical religion which helps a person in everyday affairs of life. Mere profession of Jainism is not enough, it has to be practiced and lived. As Vincent Smith, the great historian and orientalist, observed, "Jain ethics are meant for men of all positions; for kings, warriors, traders, artisans, agriculturists, and indeed for men and women in every walk of life. Do your duty, and do it as humanely as you can. This, in brief, is the primary principle of Jainism." It is a practical path, simple, easy, healthy and straight, not winding, mazy, steep, narrow or arduous. Every step forward makes the next more pleasant and joyful. Every effort towards one's own moral elevation is not only beneficial to oneself but to all those one comes in contact with. The aim of this system is the good and happiness of all without any distinction. What the Tirthankaras and the Jaina sages of yore have said has been endorsed by modern leaders of thought like Aldous Huxley, Gandhi, Nehru, Max Weber, Hermann Jacobi, Heinrich Zimmer, William Henry Talbot, George Bernard Shaw, Leonardo da Vinci and many more.

And, it is today, more than ever, when suspicion and distrust are vitiating the atmosphere of international peace and brotherhood, when the world is filled with fear and hate, that we require a living philosophy which will help us to discard them and recover ourselves. Such a living, wholesome philosophy, bearing the message of love and goodwill, ahimsā and peace, internal as well as external, personal as well as universal, is the Jaina philosophy of life. It is this system of Jaina religion, thought and culture that stands for the highest and noblest human values, moral elevation and spiritual uplift, eternal and universal peace and happiness.

— PEACE BE TO ALL —

GLOSSARY

Ācārya	Chief Pontiff; head ascetic; religious master
Ahimsa	Non-violence; non-injury (by body, mind or speech)
Ajitnath	Second Jain Tirthankara
Anekanta	Non-extremism; relativity
Aristanemi	Twenty-second Jain Thirthankara (also known as Neminath and cousin of Lord Krishna)
Arhatas	Followers of Ṛsabha (Rishabha); ancient name for Jain
Aparigraha	Non-attachment to material possessions
Artha	Entity; object; wealth
Atma	Soul; essential self
Avatara	Incarnation of a God
Bhagwan	Lord; realized soul; God
Brahamana	Caste that engages in performance of religious duties; Priestly caste
Darshana	Faith; literature; philosophy
Dharma	Meritorious qualities; duty; religion
Dravidian	Native of South India; Pre-aryan inhabitant of India
Guru	Spiritual teacher; Master
Jinas	See Tirthankara
Jnana	Knowledge; right cognizance; gnosis; mystical insight
Kama	Sensuality; indulgence in objects of touch; worldly enjoyment
Karma	Cause; deeds, good or bad, which determine one's future birth cycle

Kayotsarga	Perfect body posture; standing posture
Ksatriya	Person of warrior class
Maharishi	Monk; great sage
Mahavira	Twenty-fourth and last Jain Tirthankara, lived and preached between 599 and 527 B.C.E.
Mitra	Friend
Nirgranthas	Monks; person who is utterly devoid of the knot-of-attachment and aversion; free from bonds
Nirvana	Emancipation of the soul
Parsvanath	Twenty-third Jain Tirthankara
Path	Road; a way leading to
Pranas	Life vitalities; breath
Pandit	Scholar
Punjab	A state in the Republic of India
Puranas	Holy scriptures of Jains as well as Hindus
Rishabha	First Jain Tirthankara
Rgveda	The earliest Hindu scripture
Ṛsabha	See Rishabha
Sadhu	Monk
Sages	Virtuous persons
Saiva	Hindu sect that worships Siva
Shastras	Holy Scriptures
Smruti	Holy scriptures of Hindus
Sramanas	Listener; follower of Mahavira
Sudra	A person belonging to the lowest caste

Syadvadic	Multiple angle of observing the truth
Tirthankara	Omniscient Godman; supreme religious leader; "crossing maker" (one who has crossed over to enlightenment); a perfected human being
Unodara	To eat less
Upanishads	Hindu Holy books
Vaisnava	Hindu sect that worships Vishnu
Vaisya	Person who engages in business and commerce
Vardhamana	See Mahavira
Vedas	Collection of Hindu scriptures
Vishnu	Hindu God of Preservation
Viveka	Humililty
Vratas	Vows; solemn pledge; discipline; penance
Yajnas	Religious fire ceremony
Yati	Monks and nuns; ascetics; holy ones

Bibliography

This select bibliography includes sources from which more detailed information may be obtained. In addition to the sources listed below, the reader is directed to major universities and public libraries across North America for other published material on Jain philosophy and religion.

Barodia, U. D., **History and Literature of Jainism.** Bombay: The Jain Graduate's Association, 1909.

Buhler, Johann Georg, **The Indian Sect of the Jainas.** London: Luzac & Co., 1903.

Diwaker, S.C., **Religion and Peace.** Mathura, India: All India Digamber Jain Sangh, 1957.

Edwards, Paul, Editor in Chief, **The Encyclopedia of Philosophy.** New York: The Macmillan Co. and Free Press, 1972.

Eliade, Mircea, Editor in Chief, **The Encyclopedia of Religion.** New York: The Macmillan Publishing Co., 1986.

Giehl, Dudley, **Vegetarianism — A Way of Life.** New York: Harper and Row, 1979.

Jackson, Samuel Macauley, Editor in Chief, **Encyclopedia of Religious Knowledge.** Grand Rapids, Mich.: Baker Book House, 1967.

Jain, C. R., **Fundamentals of Jainism.** Meerut, India: Veer Nirvan Bharti, 1974.

Jain, Jyoti Prasad, **Bhagawan Mahavira: Life, Times and Teaching.** Lucknow, India: Tirthankara Mahavira Smriti Kendra Samiti, 1982.

Jain, Jyoti Prasad, **Way to Health and Happiness: Vegetarianism.** Lucknow, India: Teerthankar Mahavir Smriti Kendra Samiti, 1983.

Jain, Jyoti Prasad, **Religion and Culture of the Jains.** New Delhi: Bharatiya Jnanpith, 1977.

Jain, Kamta Prasad, **The Religion of Tirthankaras.** Aliganj (Etah), India: The World Jain Mission, 1964.

Jain, Jyoti Prasad, **Ahimsa: Right Solution of World Problems.** Aliganj (Etah), India: The World Jain Mission, 1970.

Jussawalla, J. M., **Vegetarianism.** Bombay: Somaiya Publications, 1985.

Radhakrishnan, S., **Indian Philosophy.** New York: Humanities Press, 1940.

Gommatavani (Monthly Magazine). (Shravanabelagola, India: Jain Math).

To see Jainism in action, you may write to obtain a video copy of the following documentary films:

(1) **AHIMSA — NON-VIOLENCE**
Direct Cinema, LTD
P.O. Box 69799
Los Angeles, CA 96069
Tel. (213) 652-8000

(2) **THE FRONTIERS OF PEACE**
The Visual Knowledge Corporation
Box 404
Mendham, NJ 07945
Tel. (201) 543-2000

INDEX